Building the Book
CATHEDRAL

Building the Book
CATHEDRAL

David Macaulay

HOUGHTON MIFFLIN COMPANY BOSTON 1999

Walter Lorraine Books

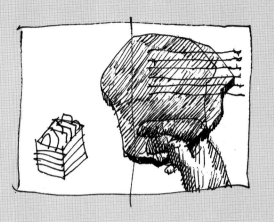

For Walter Lorraine, at last

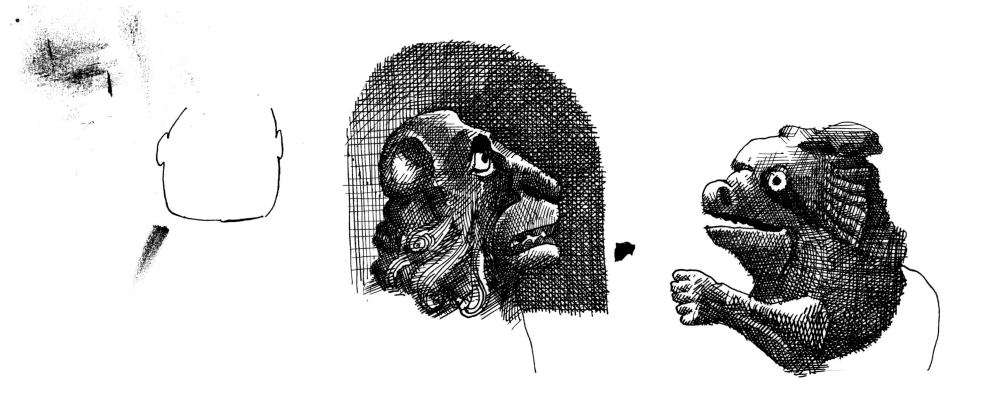

Cathedral: The Story of Its Construction turned twenty-five last year. These days just having a book in print when the old quarter-century mark rolls around is probably worth celebrating, but *Cathedral* was also my first book and remains a sentimental favorite. I did it with no particular expertise in Gothic construction and with no experience whatsoever in bookmaking. In short, for the first and last time, I worked in a state of sublime ignorance. This is the story of that fledgling effort.

Having learned a few things about bookmaking over the last two and a half decades, there was no way I could take this nostalgic journey without entertaining second thoughts about some of my early decisions. So while retelling the original story, I've taken the liberty of making a number of changes. Several drawings have moved from one page to another, and others have had their scale adjusted. A few have even been replaced by earlier sketches. But that's what I love about this process. I'm always learning.

It wasn't my idea to build a Gothic cathedral. I was just trying to make a picture book about a gargoyle beauty pageant. Over the summer of 1972, I sketched out my story and did these two drawings. That fall I showed them to Houghton Mifflin's children's book department in Boston. I'd been there before, but this time I was pretty sure I had a winner on my hands. And I guess I did. Only it wasn't the winner I had in mind. The reaction to my gargoyles was polite, mild amusement. The cathedral drawing, however, elicited real enthusiasm. Instead of declining my proposal, this time the editor offered a suggestion. "Why not tell the story of the building instead?"

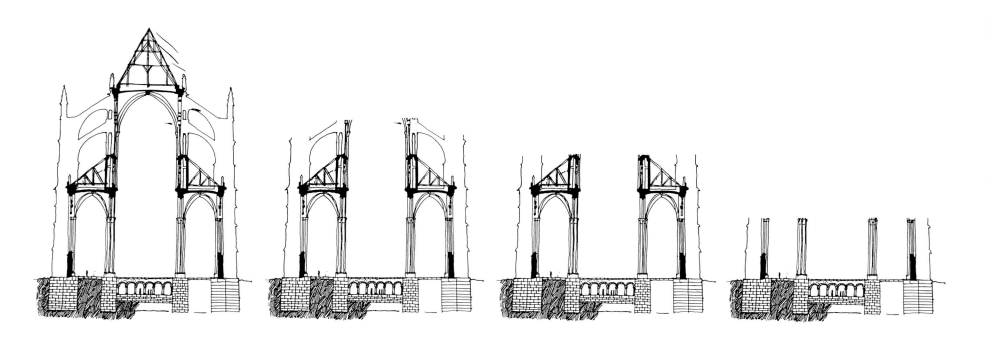

I guess I was too pleased by the encouragement to be crushed by the rejection. So the gargoyles went into seclusion and I returned to my drawing board. Not knowing exactly how to proceed, I started working over a cross section of a Gothic cathedral from one of my old textbooks. Each time I traced it, I eliminated a little more of the building, starting from the top and working my way down to the ground. When I laid the sketches in reverse order, a cathedral grew.

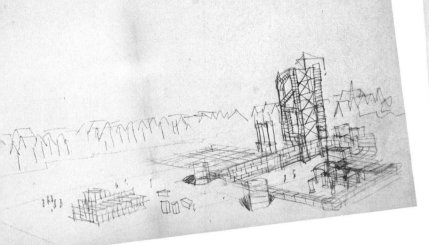

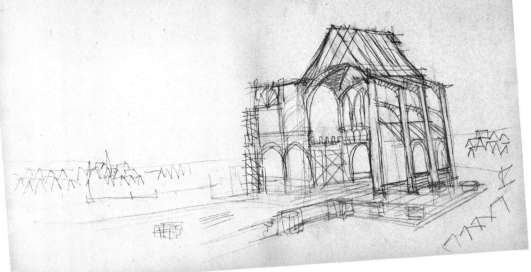

10

But it was very much a one-dimensional cathedral. So I made a second set of sketches, this time setting the building at an angle. I included all the surrounding houses to emphasize its monumental scale. When I combined both sequences, going back and forth between cross sections and overviews, I had what would become the skeleton of the book. But it still lacked a pulse, so I kept drawing. At first, I ended up with details like this one of masons at work on a stone pier.

The more I drew, the more freely I was able to move around the construction site. Eventually I came up with some sketches that although rough and full of technical inaccuracies, made me feel as if I was really there. These sketches at last began to hint at the courage and faith required of the medieval builders to erect such extraordinary structures. I made copies of all the drawings, stapled them together to create a somewhat oversize paperback book (the same size as the one you are holding now), and set off once again for the children's book department.

Not even the misspelling of my last name could diminish my excitement when a contract finally arrived. It was the third week of December 1972.

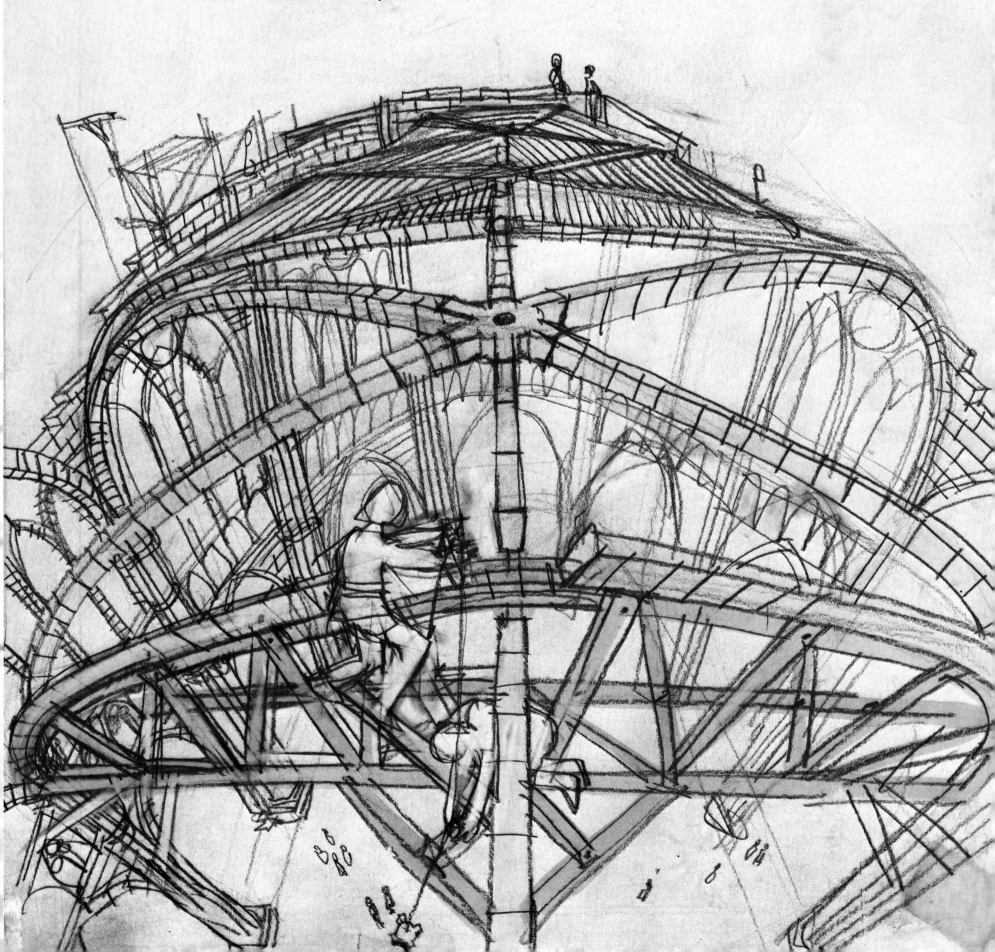

PROPOSED OUTLINE

1. WHAT IS A CATHEDRAL? WHEN WERE THEY BUILT?
2. WHY WERE THEY BUILT?
   WHAT WERE THEY MADE OF?
3. WHERE WERE THEY BUILT?
4. WHO BUILT THEM? AND WHAT TOOLS DID THEY
   a. THE CHAPTERS
   b. THE ARCHITECT/MASTER MASON
   c. THE WORKERS, THEIR JOBS AND THEIR TOOLS, THEIR
      ORGANIZATIONS.
      1. MASONS
      2. STONE CUTTERS
      3. STONE DRESSERS
      4. QUARRY MEN
      5. MORTAR MAKERS
      7. PLASTERERS
      8. PAINTERS
      9. SCULPTORS
      10. CARPENTERS
      12. GLASS BLOWERS
      13. WINDOW MAKERS
      14. ROOFERS
      15. BLACKSMITHS
      16. ROAD MAKERS
      18. LABORERS
5. HOW DID THEY BUILD A CATHEDRAL
   (over)

⑤ GETTING THE MATERIALS
A a. cutting up a lodge at the site - setting up a forge.
   b. excavating the quarry.
   c. cutting the stone out - templates
   d. dressing the stone - marking the stone for location and
      construction of roads to the
   e. transporting the stone - building site
      by water or by land.
B a. cutting wood, transportation for scaffolding.
   b. choosing a site - staking out the foundations.
   c. construction of the lodges in the workshop
   d. construction of forge
C a. excavation of foundation or holes.
   b. construction of scaffolding to remove dirt
      inclined planes carts
   e. construction of foundations - mortar makers
      metal or wooden ram to pack stone together
   f. construction of machinery to move foundation stones.
   h. construction of crypt and floor over.
   i. begin carving, sculpture and moldings and capitals.
D a. construction of scaffolding for walls - trestles, hurdles.
   b. transportation of wall stone, location of stone close to front
   c. erection of walls, opposite side - interior stairways
   d. erection of buttresses - installation of gargoyles
   e. construction of high scaffolding on top of walls
   f. putlog scaffolding - construction of cranes etc. ladders
   g. construction of flying buttress centerings on ground -
      hoist into place. locate in centerings both sides.

E a. construction of aisle rooves
   b. construction of aisle vaults.
   c. erection of mullions in window openings.
   d.

→ WINTER ←

F a. cutting timber for the main roof
   b. delivery of slate tiles or lead sheets for roofing.
   c. construction of roof on the ground - cranes on top of
      the walls
   d. hoisting up the main the beams - and locating
   e. hoisting up the great wheel in pieces - erection
      and setting up.
   f. hoisting up other beams - completion of roof
      framing.
   g. hoisting up lead sheets or slate tiles - installation.
   h. lining gutters - installation of gargoyles -

G a. construction of centering for main vault.
   b. raising centering and installation
   c. locating of ribs.
   d. laying voussoir for ribs
   e. hoisting and dropping in the keystone. flying buttresses
   f. installation of logging walls - three one layer at a time
   g. completion of webs -
   h. pouring concrete over.
   i. removal of logging -
   j. removal of centering - move to next bay.

K. move great wheel to next bay.
   l. plastering of vault
   m. painting lines on the vault web.

H a. construction of scaffolding for window construction -
   b. construction of movable platform for working on window
   c. installation of windows

I a. carving of some capitals etc. on the job
   b. painting the bosses.

   repetition of this process along the nave.

J a. construction of towers → rose window
   b. installation of sculptures -
   c. making the bells.
   d. installation of the bells -
   e. doors - hardware -

K. opening ceremony of cathedral -

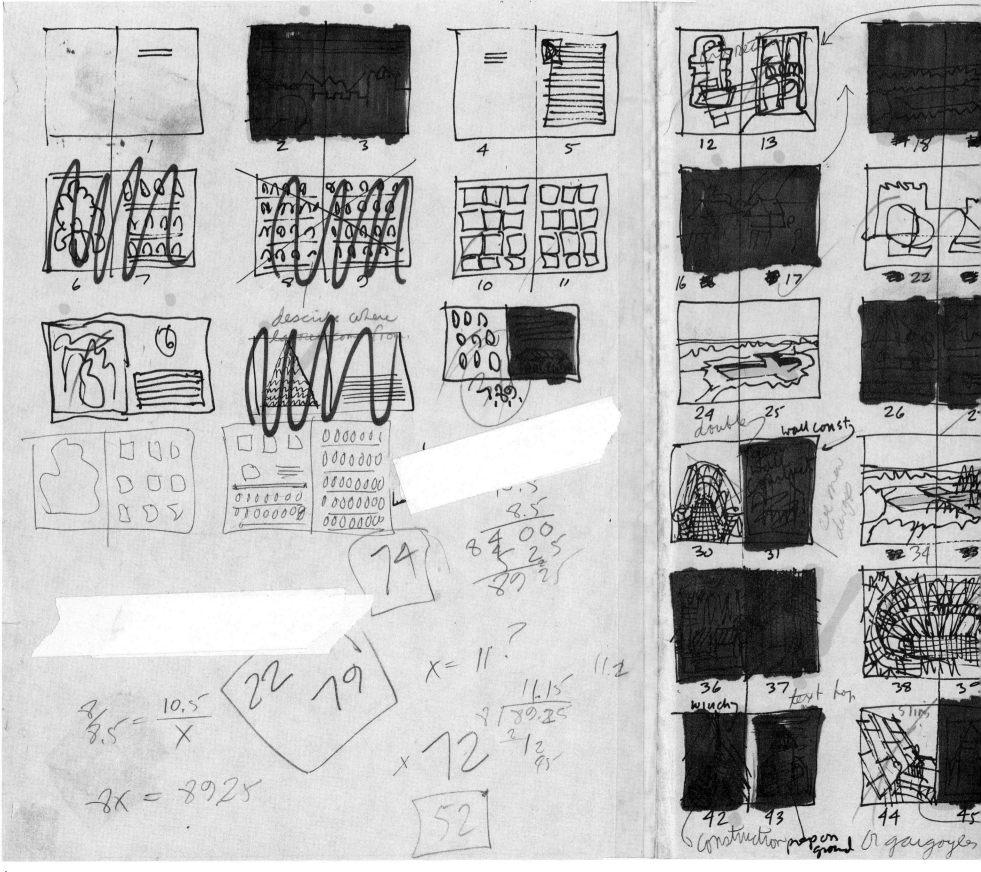

I had spent most of the month reading at the library. The more research I did, the more I realized just how much I didn't know. Even so, by mid-January the book was more or less planned out in both a rambling outline and thumbnail sketches, and it had mushroomed from thirty-three pages to eighty.

I had plenty of information to work with, and it had all come from books by people who knew a lot more about the subject than I would ever know. Still, it had been four years since I had visited a French cathedral, and here I was about to invent one. I decided I had better take another look. So in spite of a mid-March deadline, I blew half the advance and flew to France.

By the time I reached Amiens, a couple of hours north of Paris, I was exhausted. Still, I dragged my stuff off the train, dumped it at the first hotel I found, and staggered in the direction of the spire. Entering through one of the small doors cut into one of the huge doors, I found myself alone in an amazing space. I didn't draw or photograph anything. I just sat in one of the wooden chairs and stared upward, mentally dismantling the stonework above me.

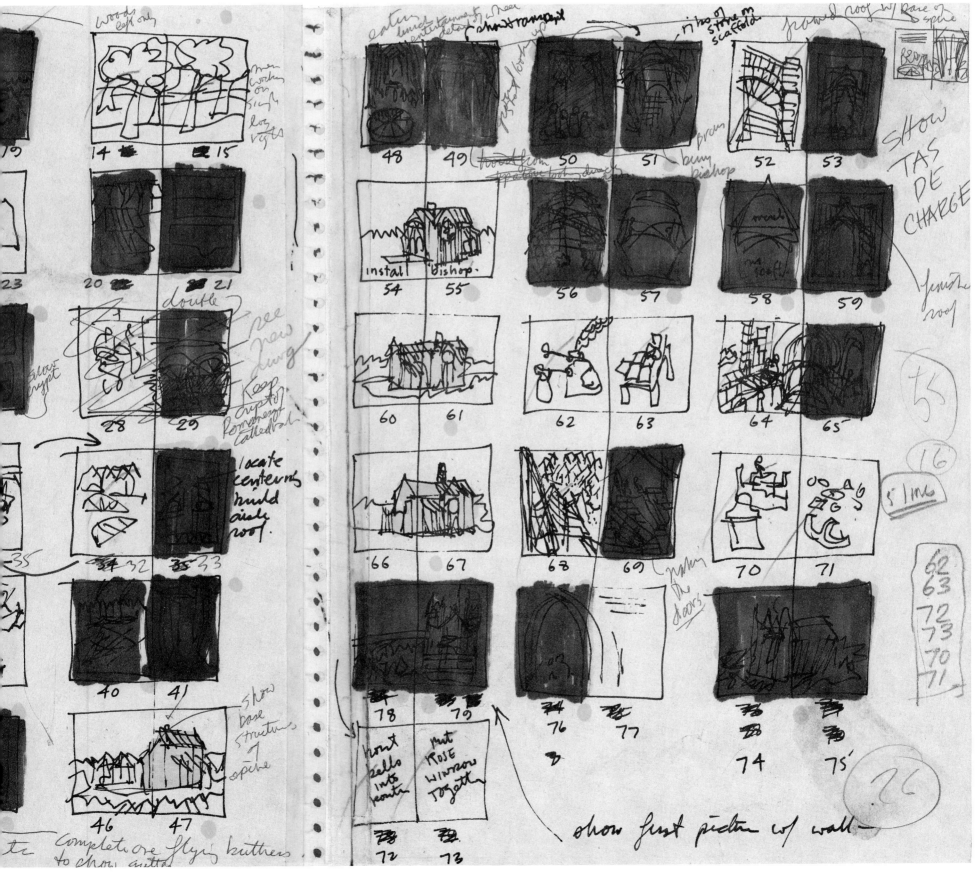

(This sketch was done at least ten years after my visit to Amiens. But it was drawn from my imagination and is based on my impressions from that cold January day.)

After an hour or so, I headed back to the hotel. In my haste to get to the cathedral, I had rented a room only slightly larger than the bed. But after an early dinner and two glasses of Muscadet, it was all I needed.

18

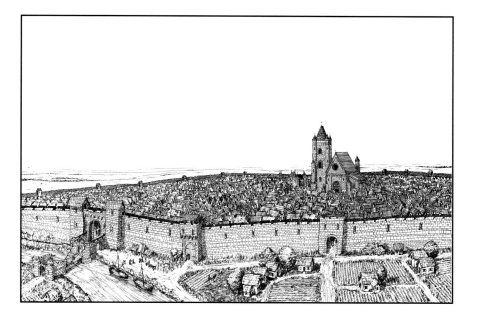

The following day, on my way back from the cathedral, I used the point and grunt method to purchase six sheets of paper, a bottle of India ink, and a couple of pens. Then I wedged myself into the space between the bed and a small round table and started drawing.

I began with the illustration of the completed façade, since I had already drawn one very much like it for the gargoyle story. I drew the title page next (because it contains the same city wall), replacing the cathedral with its Romanesque predecessor and changing the houses to show that the two scenes were roughly ninety years apart.

Finally I did the last illustration for the overview sequence. As you can see, the order in which I made the drawings was determined entirely by whether I had enough information and not at all by their final sequence. This remained true for the rest of the book.

On the second or perhaps third night, after dinner, I began the one part of the project that really intimidated me — the writing. I'd put it off for as long as possible. But now, lying on the bed, ballpoint pen in hand and using my sketches as a guide, I began inflating my trusty outline. The process was slow, but eventually the words grew into sentences and the sentences clustered into paragraphs — probably in self-defense. It took me three nights.

P S

In 1252 the people of Chutreaux decided to build a Cathedral. The longest, widest, highest and most beautiful Cathedral in all of France.

Their enthusiasm for such a project grew directly out of their love and fear of God. They had been taught by the church, for 300 years, that peace and prosperity came to their city it was a blessing directly from God. And if war or disease came to their city it was a punishment sign of Gods anger. and they must pray for mercy.

There were no wars in Chutreaux or in France for that matter.

There was no disease to speak of and there was plenty of food.

The weather had been good for the farmers, and business had been good for the merchants. There were great Such Blessings, the people of Chutreaux wished to thank God, before he changed his mind. And what better way to thank him than to build Him a Cathedral.

Also, a Cathedral would be a more worthy resting place for the sacred remains of St. Gulbirth, a knight whose skull and fore finger had been sent back from Constantinople by Louis IX during the 7th Crusade. and presented to the Bishop.

Such relics were worshipped by all the people of Chutreaux and indeed all the people of Europe.

Another reason for such an undertaking was that lightning had just struck and burned severely damaged the old cathedral.

Possibly there was one more reason. — The people of nearby Amiens, Rouen and Beauvais were themselves in the process of building magnificent Cathedrals. The people of Chutreaux would not knowingly be outdone — on earth especially or in heaven.

Although the Bishop was the head of the Church in Chutreaux it was the members of the chapter who controlled the money. They hired the architect William of Planz to design and supervise the construction of their Cathedral. He then chose the master Craftsmen to work under him.

The master quarryman, the master stone cutter, the sculptor, the mortar maker, the master mason, the master carpenter, the blacksmith the roofer and the glass maker.

Each master craftsman ran a work shop for his own particular trade. He had many apprentices, men who were learning the trade in hopes of one day become masters themselves. But most of the heavy work was done by laborers. These were men with no particular skill. Some came from Chutreaux, some were workers their way back from the crusades for their freedom. others were runaway slaves working until they became free.

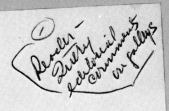

A CATHEDRAL FOR CHUTREAUX

For hundreds of years the people of Europe were taught by the church that God was the most important force in a man's life. If a man prospered, he thanked God for his kindness. If a man suffered, he begged for God's mercy, for surely God was punishing him.

In the thirteenth century God had been good to the people of France and especially to the people of Chutreaux. They had no wars to fight and the plague was gone. The weather was good for the farmers so there was plenty of food to eat. Business was good for the city's merchants. For these blessings and to help insure that He would continue to favor them the city of Chutreaux wished to thank God. They people began to dream of building Him a new Cathedral.

A new cathedral would offer a worthy resting place for the sacred remains of St. Germain. He was a knight whose skull and forefinger had been sent back from Constantinople by Louis IX during the seventh Crusade. Such relics as these were worshipped by people throughout Europe. Also at the time the people of nearby Amiens, Beauvais, and Rouen were building new cathedrals. The people of Chutreaux did not wish to be outdone, on earth or especially in heaven.

The final decision to build a new cathedral was made in the year 1252 after lightening struck and severely damaged the old cathedral. The people of Chutreaux would build the longest, widest, highest and most beautiful cathedral in all of France. The new cathedral would be built to the glory of God and it mattered little that it might take more than one hundred years to construct it.

5

A week later I was back home typing the manuscript — a humanitarian gesture — to send off for editing. When I got my little story back, however, it looked like a war casualty. The pages had been invaded by questions. Apparently I hadn't been quite as lucid in France as I had thought. I carefully picked my way through this editorial minefield, clarifying, double-checking, and rewriting.

As soon as the manuscript was finished, again I turned my full and undivided attention to the drawings. The drafting table was cleared. A revised layout of thumbnail sketches was taped to the wall to guide me. I had plenty of ink and paper and was wearing my favorite brown sweater. In short, I was ready. The score was three down, fifty-seven to go.

CATHEDRAL

The Story of It's Construction

DAVID MACAULAY

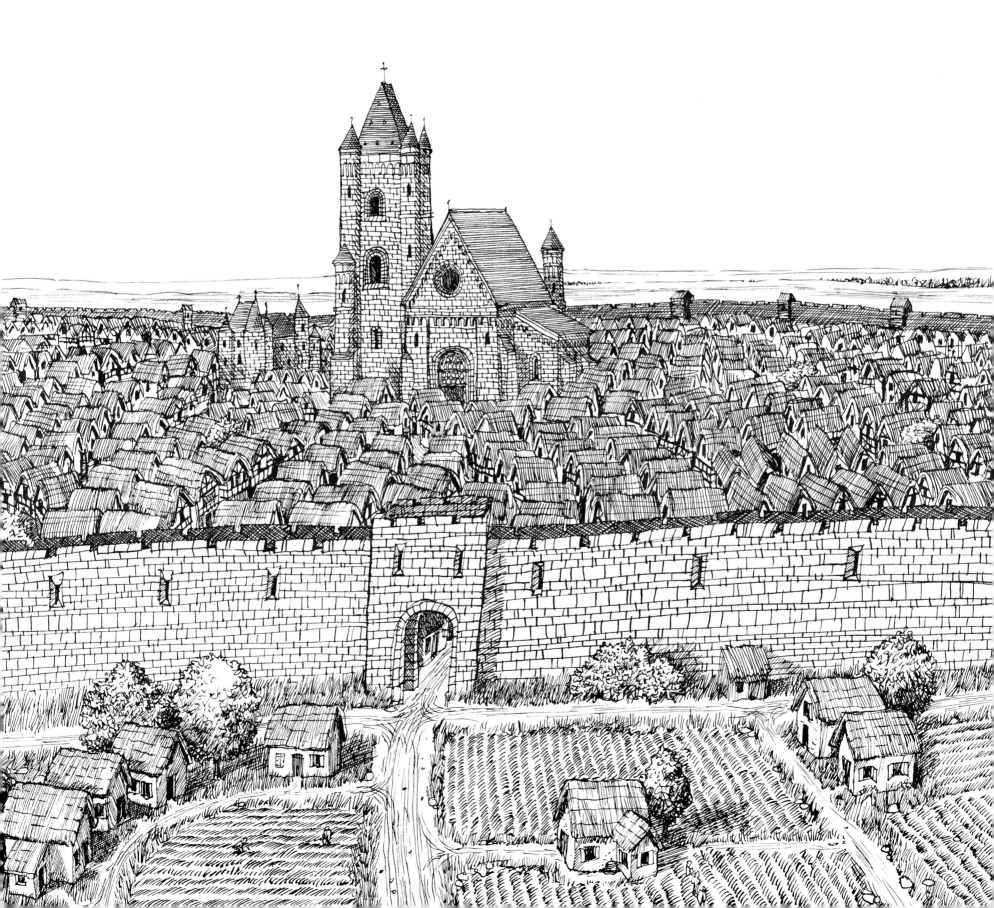

To make my fictional town seem as authentic as possible, I invented the French-sounding name Chutreaux. In an epilogue to the first draft, the town and its magnificent cathedral were still standing until the Second World War, when both were inadvertently bombed to smithereens. In the end this seemed an unnecessarily complicated (not to mention depressing) way of saying "Don't go looking for the place. I made it up."

Galley FIVE

T8565   Houghton Mifflin   10-420-10   2-27-73   GR

1	2	3	4	5	6	7	8	9	10	11	12	13	14	15
16	17	18	19	20	21	22	23	24	25	26	27	28		
29	30	31	32	33	34	35	36	37	38	39	40	41		
42	43	44	45	46	47	48	49	50	51	52	53	54		
55	56	57	58	59	60	61	62	63	64	65	66	67		
68	69	70	71	72	73	74	75	76	77	78	79	80		

T8565 Houghton Mifflin   10-420-10   3-20-73   RL

PREFACE

The cathedral of Chutreaux is imaginary, but the methods of its construction correspond closely to the actual construction of a Gothic cathedral. The story of its almost uninterrupted construction, however, represents a somewhat ideal situation. For owing to either financial or structual problems or both, the completion of many such undertakings was delayed for as long as two hundred years.

Although the people of Chutreaux are imaginary, their single-mindedness, their spirit, and their incredible courage are typical of the people of twelfth-, thirteenth-, and fourteenth-century Europe whose magnificent dreams still stand today.

For hundreds of years the people of Europe were taught by the church that God was the most important force in their lives. If they prospered, they thanked God for His kindness. If they suffered, they begged for God's mercy, for surely God was punishing them.

In the thirteenth century God was good to the people of France and especially to the people of Chutreaux. They had no wars to fight and the plague was gone. The weather was good for the farmers so there was plenty of food to eat, and business was good for the city's merchants. For these blessings and to help insure that He would continue to favor them, the city of Chutreaux wished to thank God. The people began to dream of building Him a new cathedral.

A new cathedral would offer a worthy resting place for the sacred remains of Saint Germain, a knight of the First Crusade whose skull and forefinger had later been sent back from Constantinople by Louis IX. Such relics as these were worshipped by people throughout Europe. And a new cathedral was an attractive idea for yet another reason. At the time the people of nearby Amiens, Beauvais, and Rouen were building new cathedrals. The people of Chutreaux did not wish to be outdone, on earth or especially in heaven.

The final decision to build a new cathedral was made in the year 1252, after lightning struck and severely damaged the old cathedral. The people of Chutreaux wished to build the longest, widest, highest, and most beautiful cathedral in all of France. The new cathedral would be built to the glory of God and it mattered little that it might take more than one hundred years to construct it.

Although the bishop was the head of the church in Chutreaux, it was the group of clergymen known as the chapter who controlled the money. It was the chapter who hired the Flemish architect William of Planz. William had gained his knowledge of architecture and engineering by visiting and working on many cathedrals not only in France but also in England and Germany. His reputation as an excellent master builder had reached Chutreaux through the returning crusaders. So he was summoned by the chapter to design and supervise the construction of the new cathedral, and to hire the master craftsmen who would work under him.

Master builder William of Planz was clearly a man ahead of his time. In this early sketch he is holding what appears to be blueprints. He could have used parchment, but building plans were also drawn on either plaster or right on the stone floor, neither of which rolls up easily. So I gave him a compass instead.

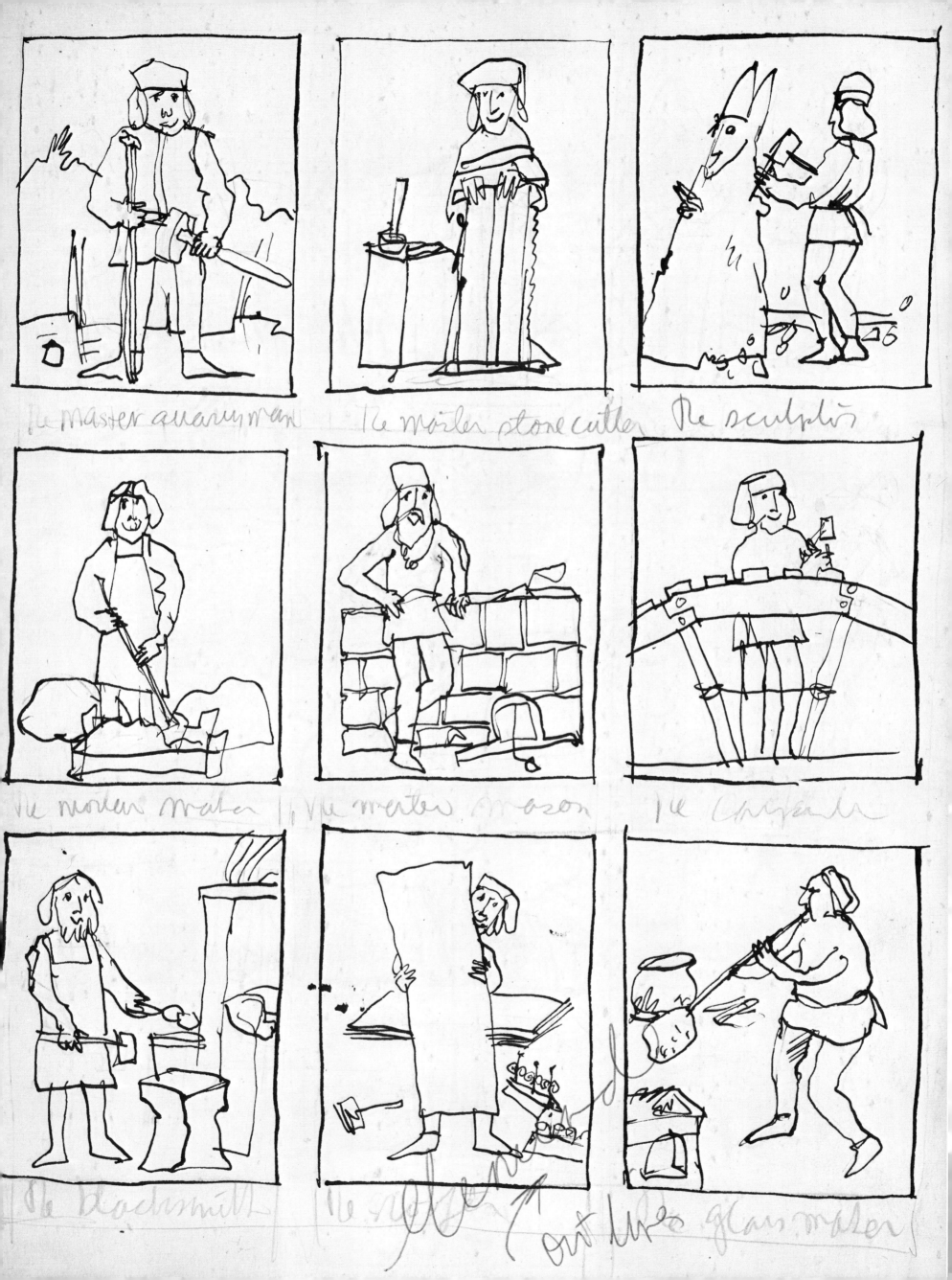

The master quarryman   The master stonecutter   The sculptor

The mortar maker   The master mason   The carpenter

The blacksmith   The _____   out like glass maker

The craftsmen were the master quarryman, the master stone cutter, the master sculptor, the master mortar maker, the master mason, the master carpenter, the master blacksmith, the master roofer, and the master glass maker.

Each master craftsman ran a workshop for his own particular trade. He had many apprentices or assistants who were learning the trade in hopes of one day becoming masters themselves. Most of the heavy work was done by laborers, men with no particular skill. Some came from Chutreaux, some from the surrounding countryside, and some were working their way back from the Crusades.

I have replaced the original left-hand page with this early sketch to show that drawing more lines doesn't necessarily improve an illustration. Look at the guys above and you'll see what I mean.

Pickaxe

Hammer

Chisel

Template

Lever

Measuring Stick

Square

Saw

Dividers

30

Each workshop required specific tools. All the metal tools were made by a blacksmith, and the wooden pieces were made by skilled woodworkers. The two main workshops, and those that required the most tools, were the stone cutters' workshop and the carpenters' workshop.

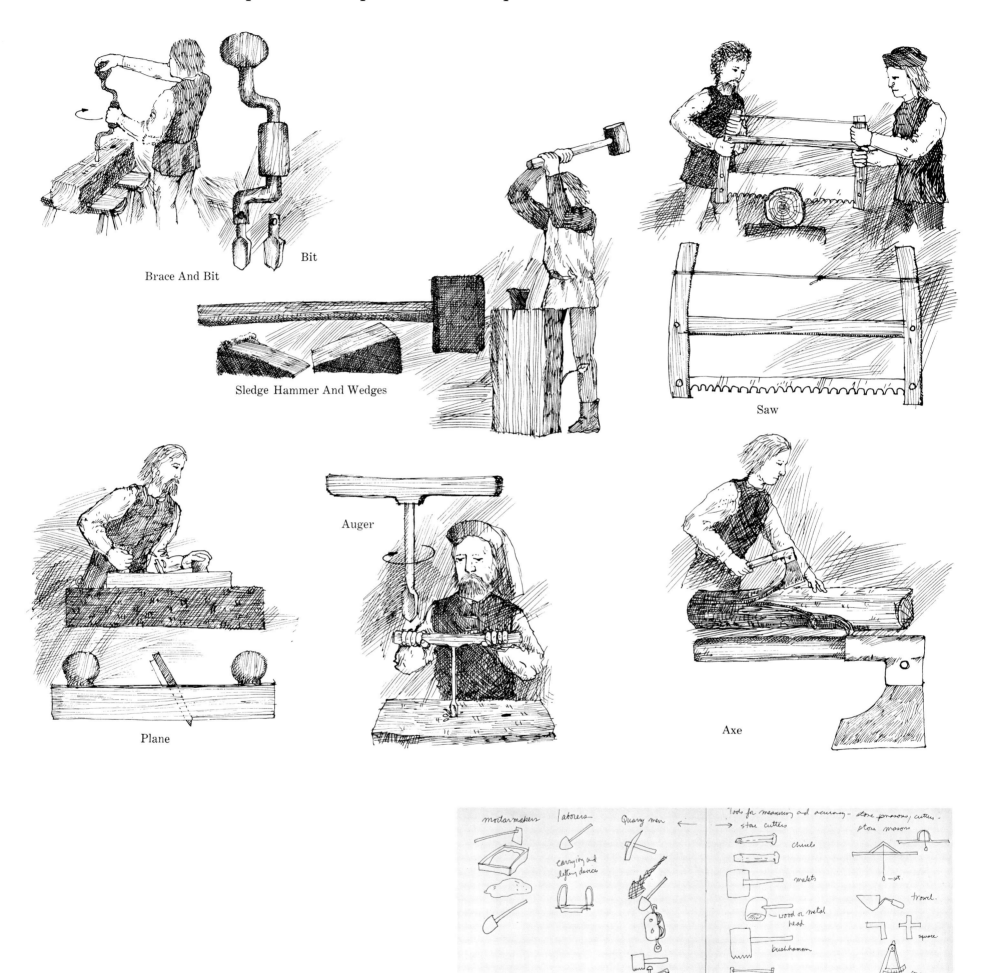

Brace And Bit

Bit

Sledge Hammer And Wedges

Saw

Auger

Plane

Axe

I realized it would be more useful to show the various tools being used rather than simply cataloging them as in my sketchbook. But for some reason my masons seem slightly happier than my carpenters. Perhaps they belong to a better union.

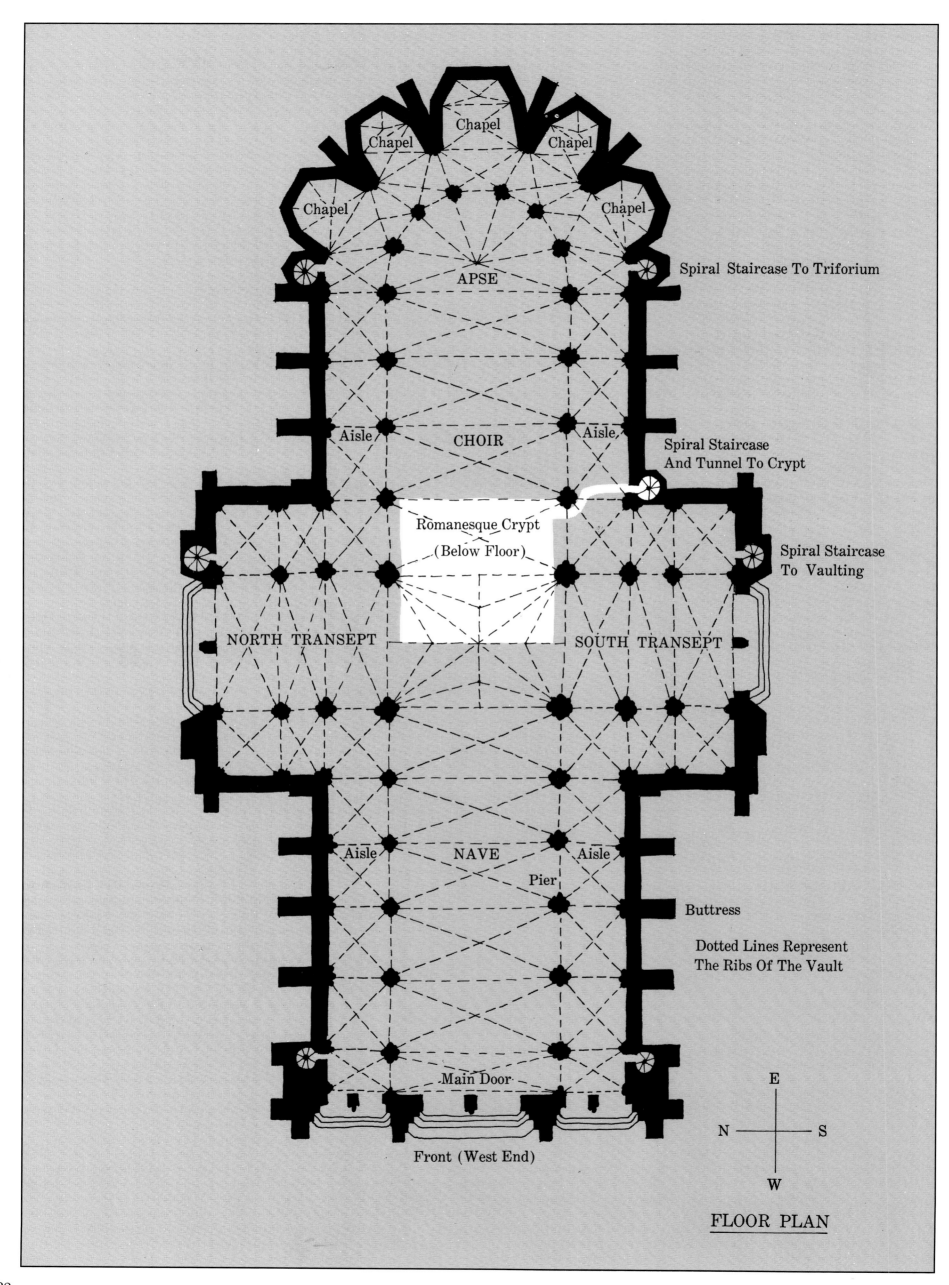

Chapel

Chapel

Chapel

Chapel

Chapel

APSE

Spiral Staircase To Triforium

Aisle

CHOIR

Aisle

Spiral Staircase
And Tunnel To Crypt

Romanesque Crypt

(Below Floor)

Spiral Staircase
To Vaulting

NORTH TRANSEPT

SOUTH TRANSEPT

Aisle

NAVE

Aisle

Pier

Buttress

Dotted Lines Represent
The Ribs Of The Vault

Main Door

E

N ——— S

W

Front (West End)

FLOOR PLAN

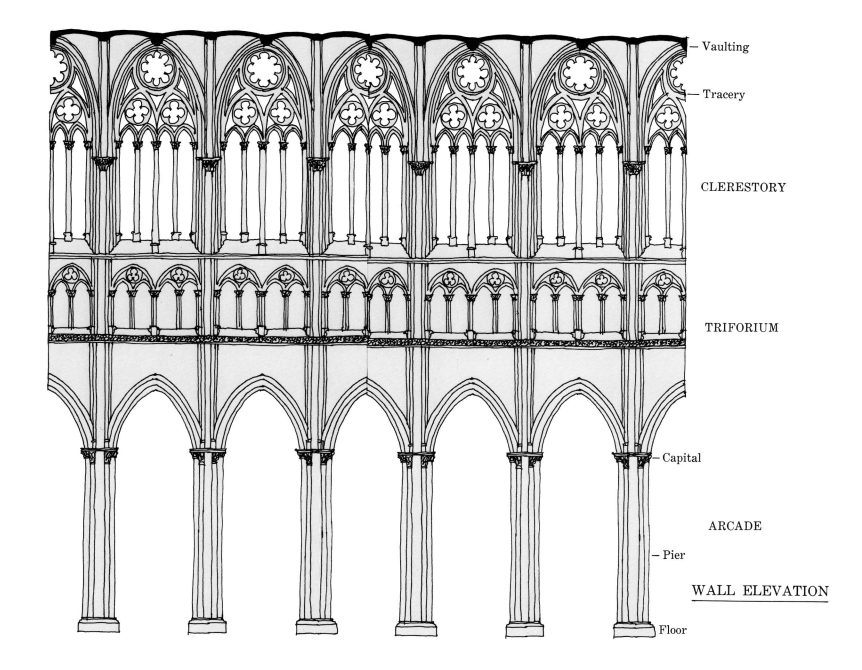

Vaulting

Tracery

CLERESTORY

TRIFORIUM

Capital

ARCADE

Pier

<u>WALL ELEVATION</u>

Floor

In the following weeks William planned and sketched and eventually settled on his final design. He combined methods and details from the cathedrals he had seen in his travels with his instruction from the chapter to design the longest, widest, highest, and most beautiful cathedral possible. The final designs were drawn on two sheets of plaster and presented to the bishop and the chapter. On one a floor plan was drawn that showed the layout of the cathedral naming all the different areas. The second had an elevation of one wall showing the different parts of the cathedral from the ground to the topmost vault.

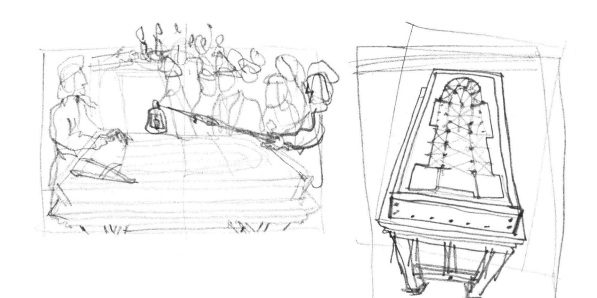

At first I considered showing the plans as if drawn on plaster and set on a table for the chapter to see. Presenting them this way instead makes them easier to read, and we become the chapter.

Once the design had been approved, the master carpenter and his apprentices, along with one hundred and fifty laborers, were sent into the forest of Chantilly. Here the master carpenter supervised the cutting of timber for the construction of scaffolding, workshops, and machines.

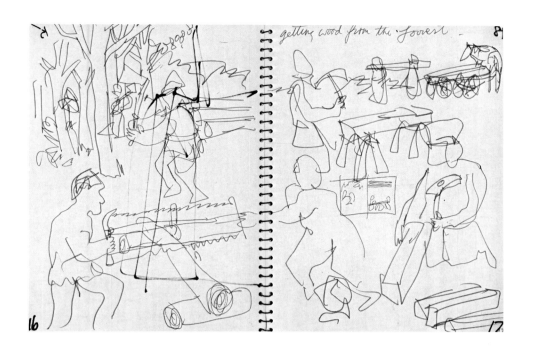

At first I was going to show all the workers laboring away in the forest. But seeing how much of the forest had to be cut down for the project turned out to be more dramatic. And besides, tree stumps are a lot easier to draw than people.

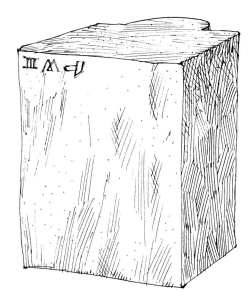

At the same time, the master quarryman was sent to supervise fifty apprentice stone cutters and two hundred and fifty laborers who would work in the Somme valley, an area known for its limestone.

A workshop was built for the stone cutters along with a forge, where the blacksmith could make new tools to replace the old ones as they wore out. Laborers helped the stone cutters lift large pieces of stone out of the quarry. Then the stone was cut, chiseled, and hammered by the stone cutters so it would match the patterns or templates supplied by the master mason. Each stone was marked three times, once to show its future location in the cathedral, once to show which quarry it came from — so that the quarry man would be paid for every stone he extracted — and once to show which stone cutter had actually cut the stone, so that he would be paid as well.

Working in black and white is a very forgiving way of entering the world of illustration. When I made a mistake or changed my mind, I just stuck a piece of paper over the problem and drew right on top of it. Attempting to add a little comic relief to the quarry scene, I included a sleeping worker and a disgruntled foreman. Unfortunately, the idea was better than the execution, so I covered them up. If you look carefully, you can just make out the shape of the patch. So much for comedy.

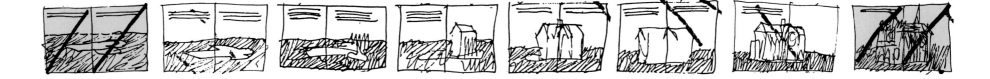

On May 24, 1252, laborers began clearing the actual site for the new cathedral. The ruins of the old cathedral were demolished except for the crypt, where the former bishops of Chutreaux lay buried. As the new cathedral was to be much larger, many houses were removed and even part of the bishop's palace was torn down. Once the east end of the site had been cleared, the location of the apse and choir was marked out with wooden stakes.

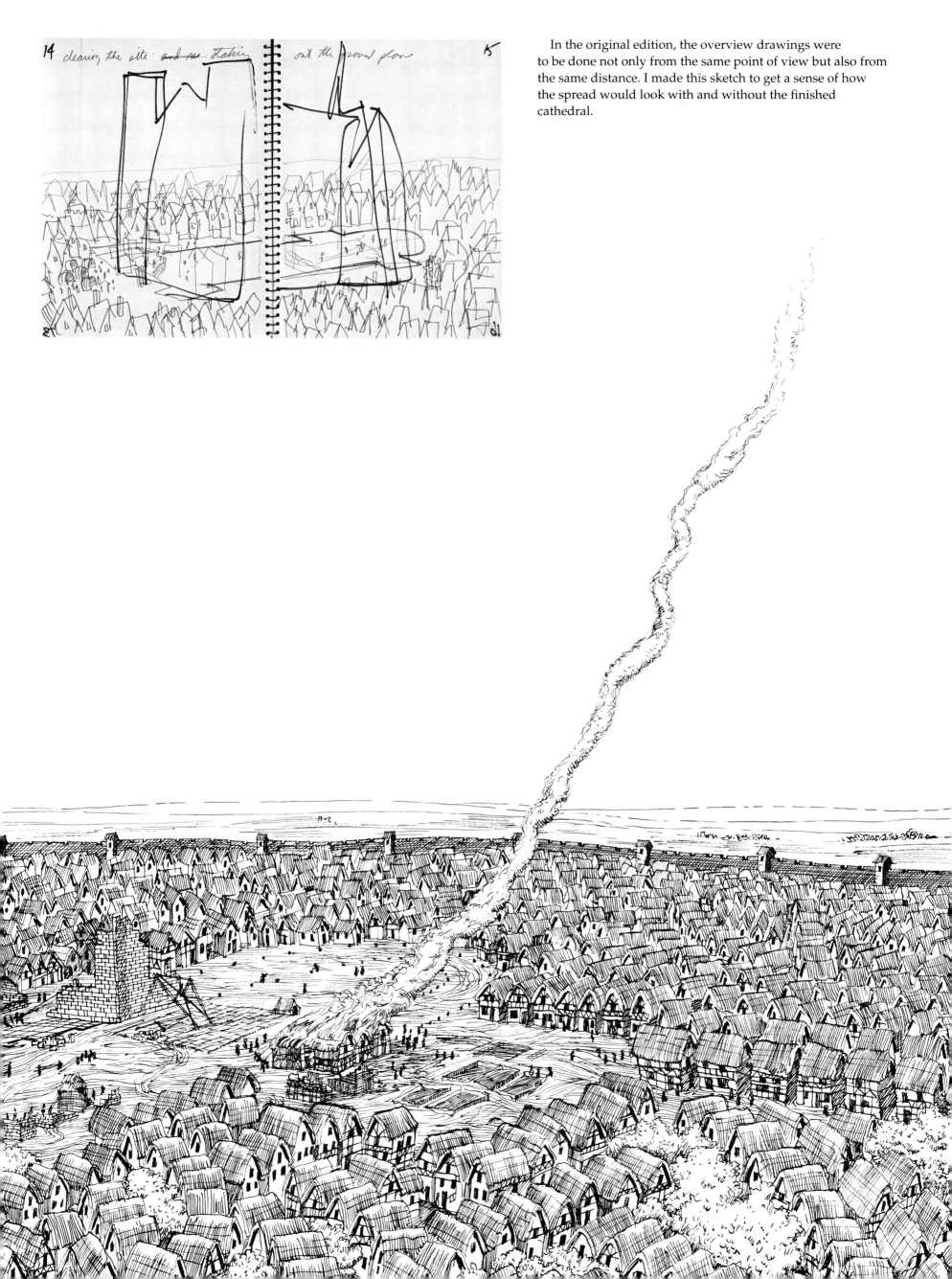

In the original edition, the overview drawings were to be done not only from the same point of view but also from the same distance. I made this sketch to get a sense of how the spread would look with and without the finished cathedral.

Workshops were built where the craftsmen could eat, rest, and work in bad weather. Another forge was built for the production of tools and nails. Finally the laborers began to dig the hole for the foundation. The foundation was to be made of thick walls, built twenty-five feet below ground level, which would support the building and prevent it from settling unevenly.

The forge in this little sketch was all the information I had for the blacksmith's shop. So I set it up in a one-and-a-half-car garage, threw in some tools for authenticity and some animals for amusement, and just hoped no one would park there.

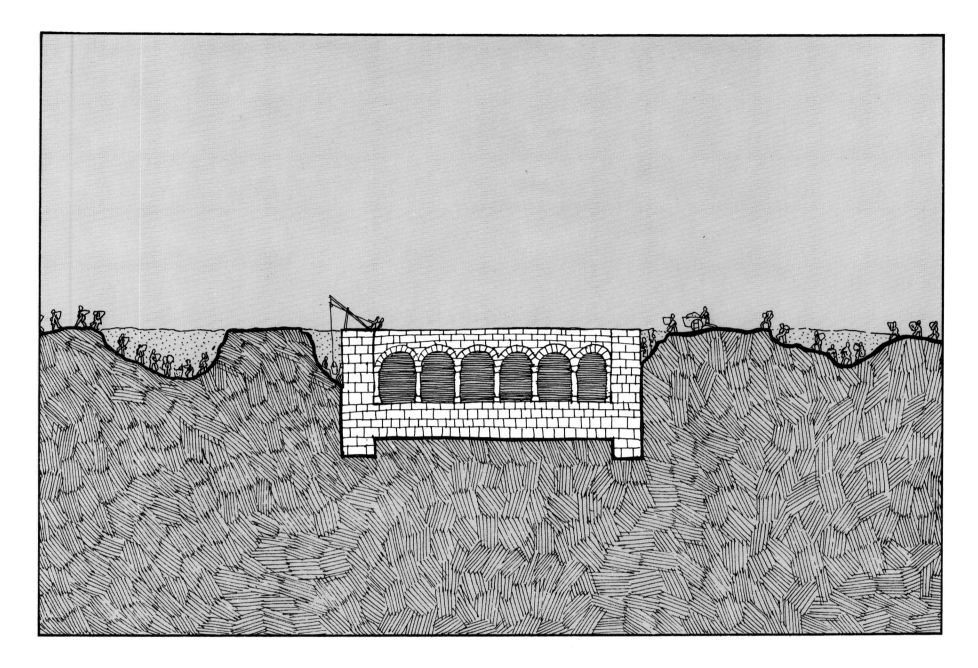

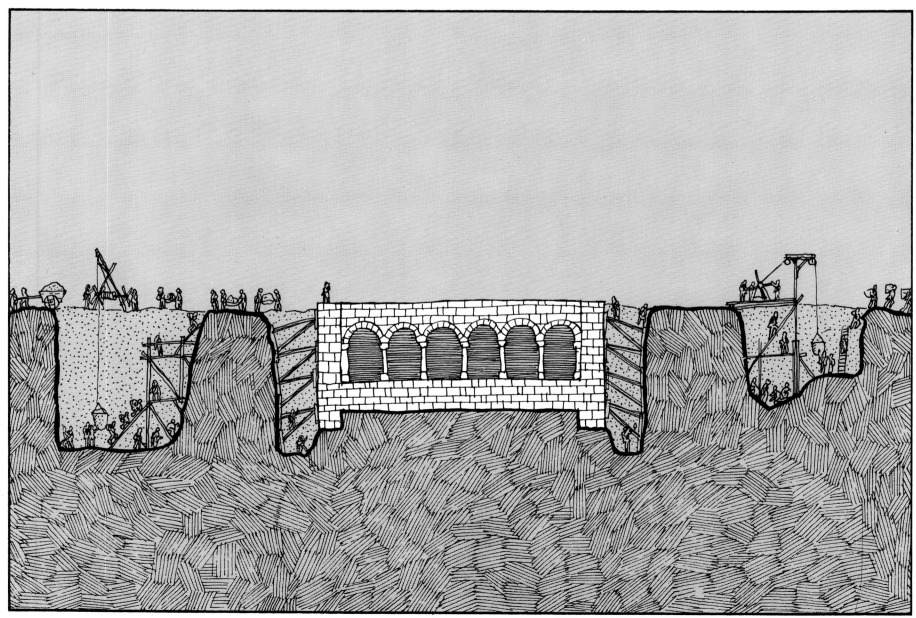

For the construction of the roof, large pieces of wood, some sixty feet long, had to be ordered from Scandinavia. Soon the wood and stone, which had been floated down the river from the quarry, began to arrive at the city's port. They were hoisted out of the boats with derricks and windlasses built by the carpenters and put into waiting carts that carried them through the town to the site.

On a good day, the design of a page doesn't change much from the earliest sketch to the finished illustration. Unfortunately, there aren't that many good days.

For the construction of the roof, large pieces of wood, some sixty feet long, had to be ordered from Scandinavia. Soon the wood and stone, which had been floated down the river from the quarry, began to arrive at the city's port. They were hoisted out of the boats with derricks and windlasses built by the carpenters and put into waiting carts that carried them through the town to the site.

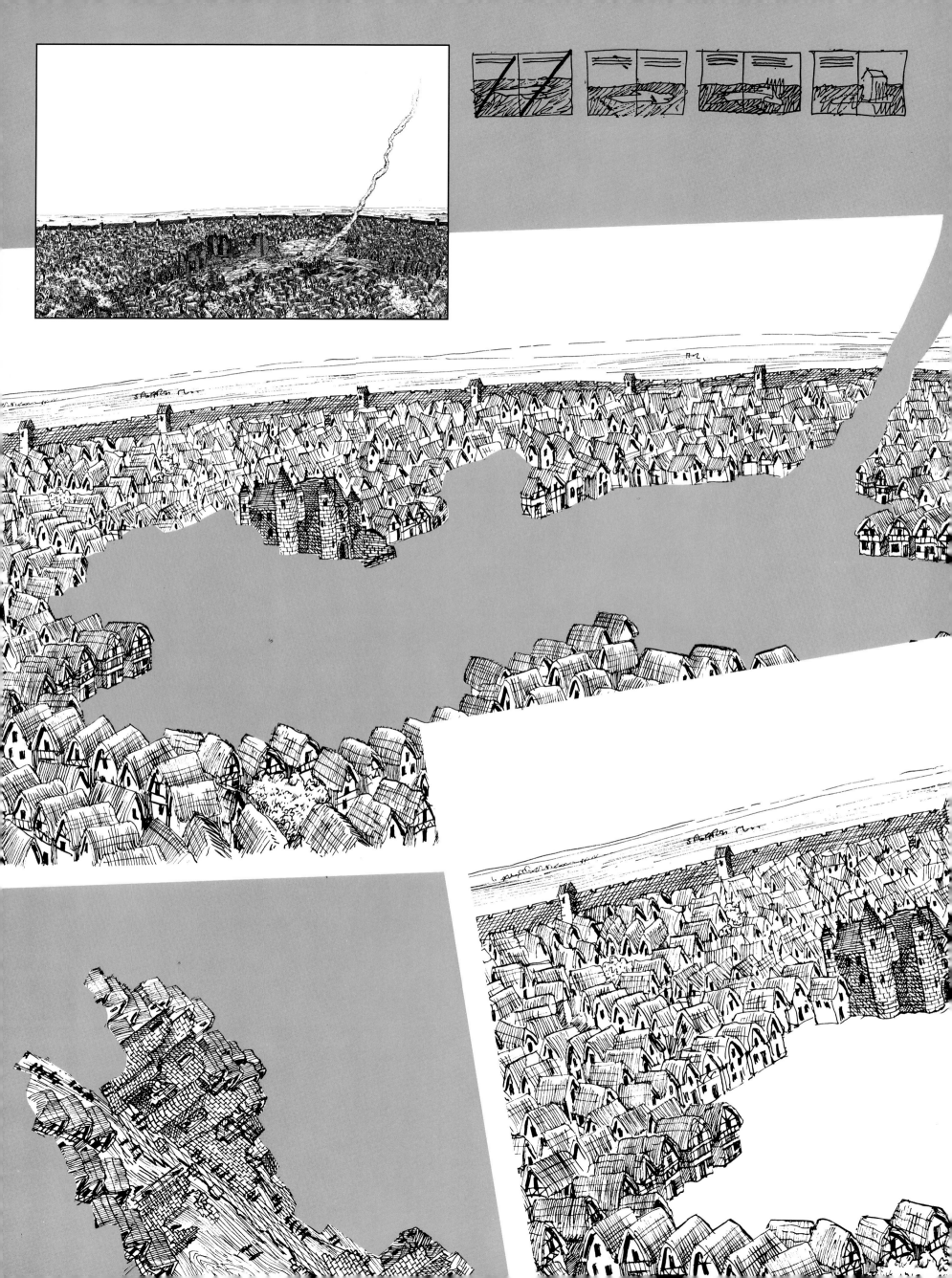

Step one: On a photo print of drawing number one, cut out the section that needs to be changed.

Step two: Discard it.

Step three: Fasten the remaining photo print to a clean piece of drawing paper.

Step four: Fill in the missing bits.

Only the first and last overview illustrations were drawn in their entirety. Numbers two, three, and four were made by patching over photo prints of number one. Five, six, and seven were made over photo prints of number eight. Although this technique guaranteed consistency and saved a lot of time, it was not entirely problem free. As you'll see on the next page, one of the towers along the city wall inadvertently disappeared when I eliminated the smoke.

By mid November the foundation hole for the apse and choir had been completely excavated.

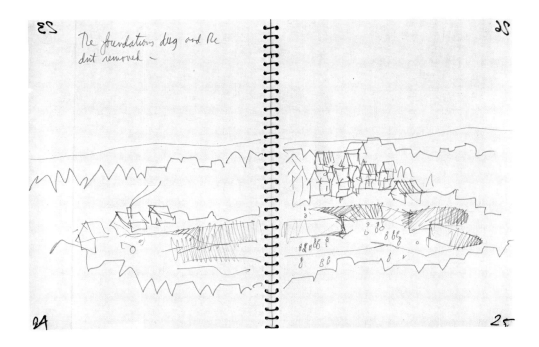

The foundations dug and the dirt removed —

I don't know what I was thinking when I made this sketch. First of all, I had forgotten about the crypt from the old church, which would need to be incorporated into the new structure. Second, each of the various foundations would have its own individual trench. What I blithely envisioned here would have been the largest known municipal swimming pool in all of medieval Europe (not to mention the first) and would have entailed removing enough dirt to bury half of Paris.

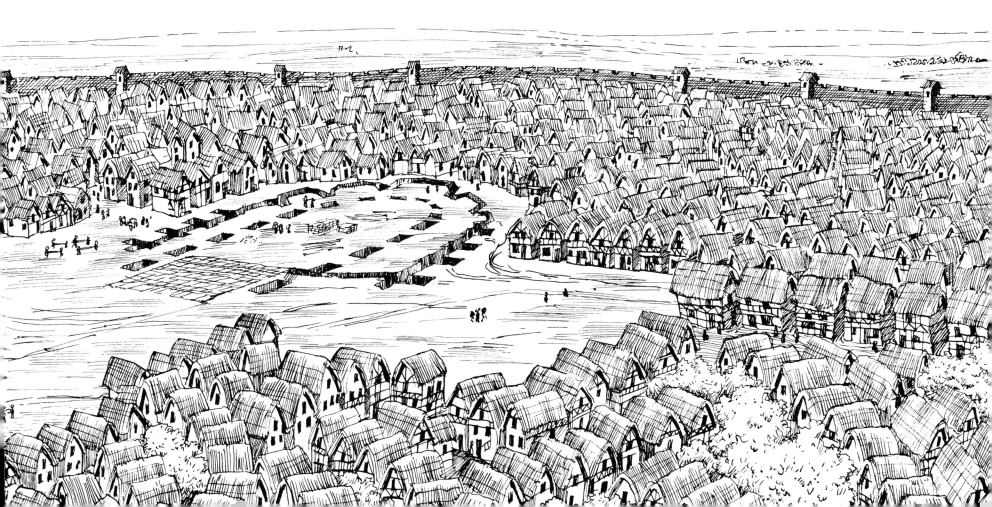

show master mason at work overseeing the operation

P 26

On April 14, 1253, the bishop of Chutreaux blessed the first foundation stone as it was lowered onto the bed of small stones covering the clay at the bottom of the excavation.

The mortar men were ready with exact mixtures of sand, lime, and water. Laborers carried the mortar down the ladders to the masons who would lay the stones on top of each other, troweling a layer of mortar between each stone and each layer of stones. When it was dry the mortar would permanently bind the stones together.

The master mason checked continually with his level to make sure the stones were perfectly horizontal and with his plumb line to make sure that the wall was perfectly vertical. Any mistake in the foundation could endanger the wall that was to be built on top of it.

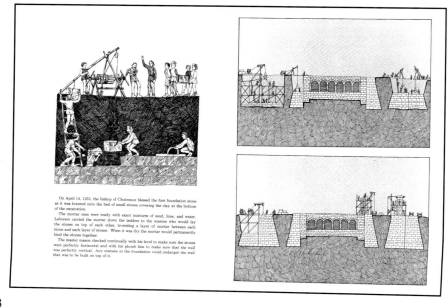

In trying to figure out how best to show the foundations, I went back and forth between an elevation and something more three-dimensional. Just for variety, I should have stayed with the three-dimensional approach, since I already had an elevation on the opposite page. But there was also a technical problem. In my earliest sketches, I showed the foundations as vertical walls instead of pyramid shaped. Fortunately, I discovered the error in time.

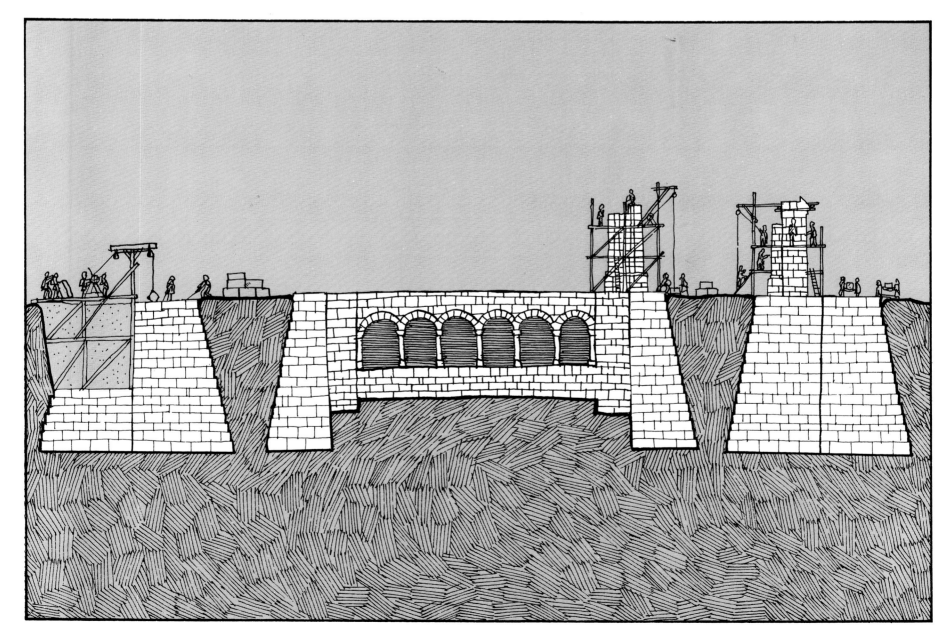

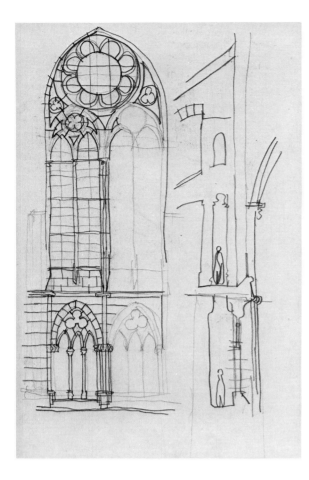

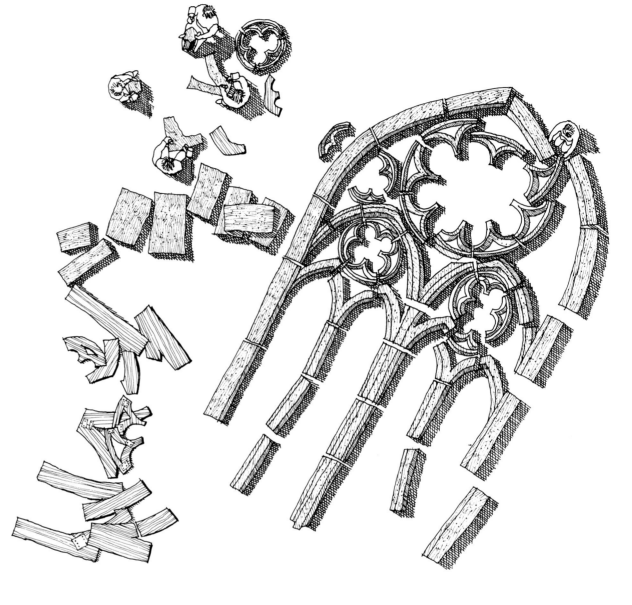

When the foundation was complete, work began on the walls. The walls of a Gothic cathedral like Chutreaux's consist of the piers or columns that support the vault and roof, and the space between the piers that is filled for the most part with the tracery — the stone framework of the windows — and small areas of solid-wall construction. The piers of the choir at Chutreaux were to be one hundred and sixty feet high and six to eight feet thick. They were constructed of hundreds of pieces of cut stone. The tracery, all of which was cut from templates, was cemented into place along with iron reinforcing bars as the piers were being built.

For the small areas of solid wall the stone mason would actually construct two parallel walls of cut stone. Then, using a piece of wood or chain as reinforcement, he would fill the space between them with concrete, a mixture of mortar and small stones. It would have been too expensive to build walls of solid stone.

The architect knew that buttresses had to be built to relieve the pressure the vault would place on the piers. These buttresses, erected on foundations next to the piers, would later be connected to the piers themselves by stone arches known as flying buttresses. In Gothic cathedrals the arched vault tended to push the piers outward. This force was transferred through the flying buttress to the buttress itself and then down to the foundation. In this way the main piers could remain quite thin in proportion to their height, allowing more space for the windows between them.

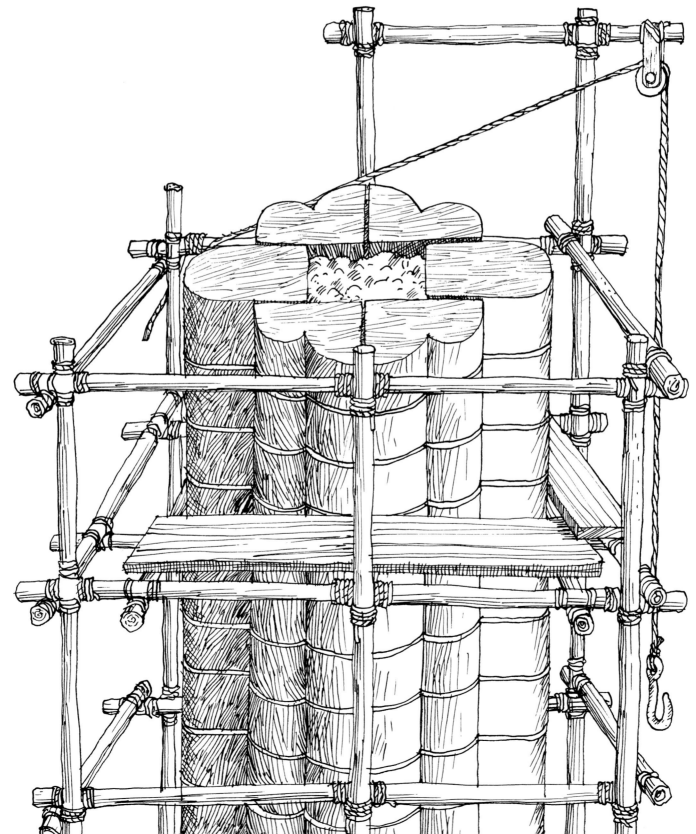

As the walls grew higher wooden scaffolding became a necessity. The scaffolding was made of poles lashed together with rope. Hoists were attached to it so that the stones and mortar could be lifted. The scaffolds also held work platforms for the masons made of mats of woven twigs. They were called hurdles and could be easily moved.

Since long pieces of wood were both difficult to find and expensive, the scaffolding for the walls above the arcade did not reach to the ground. It was hung from the walls and lifted as construction progressed. Ladders were not necessary to reach it, as several permanent spiral staircases were built into the wall itself.

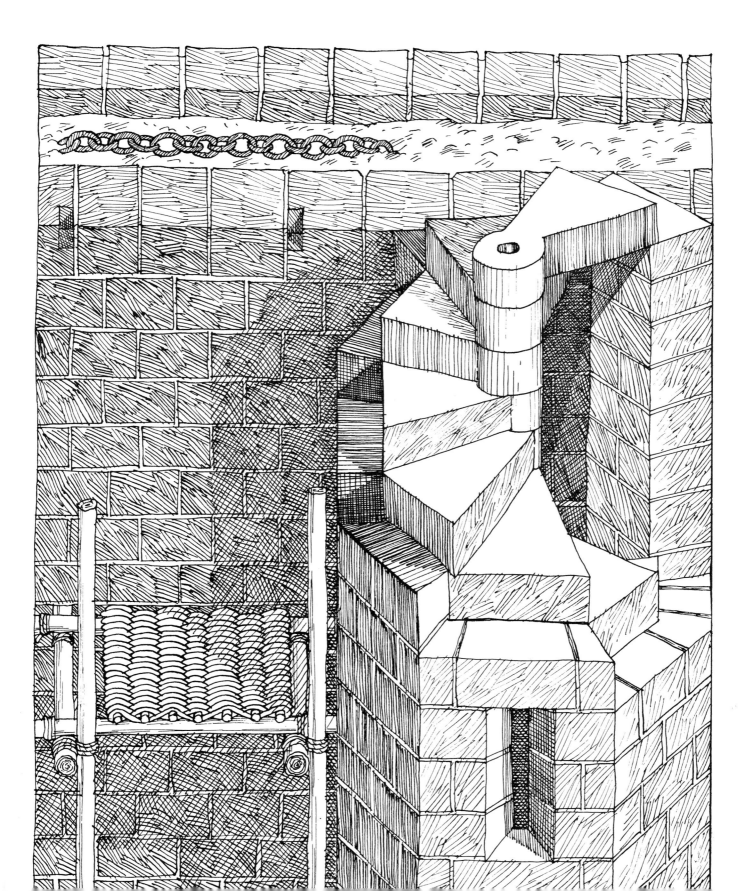

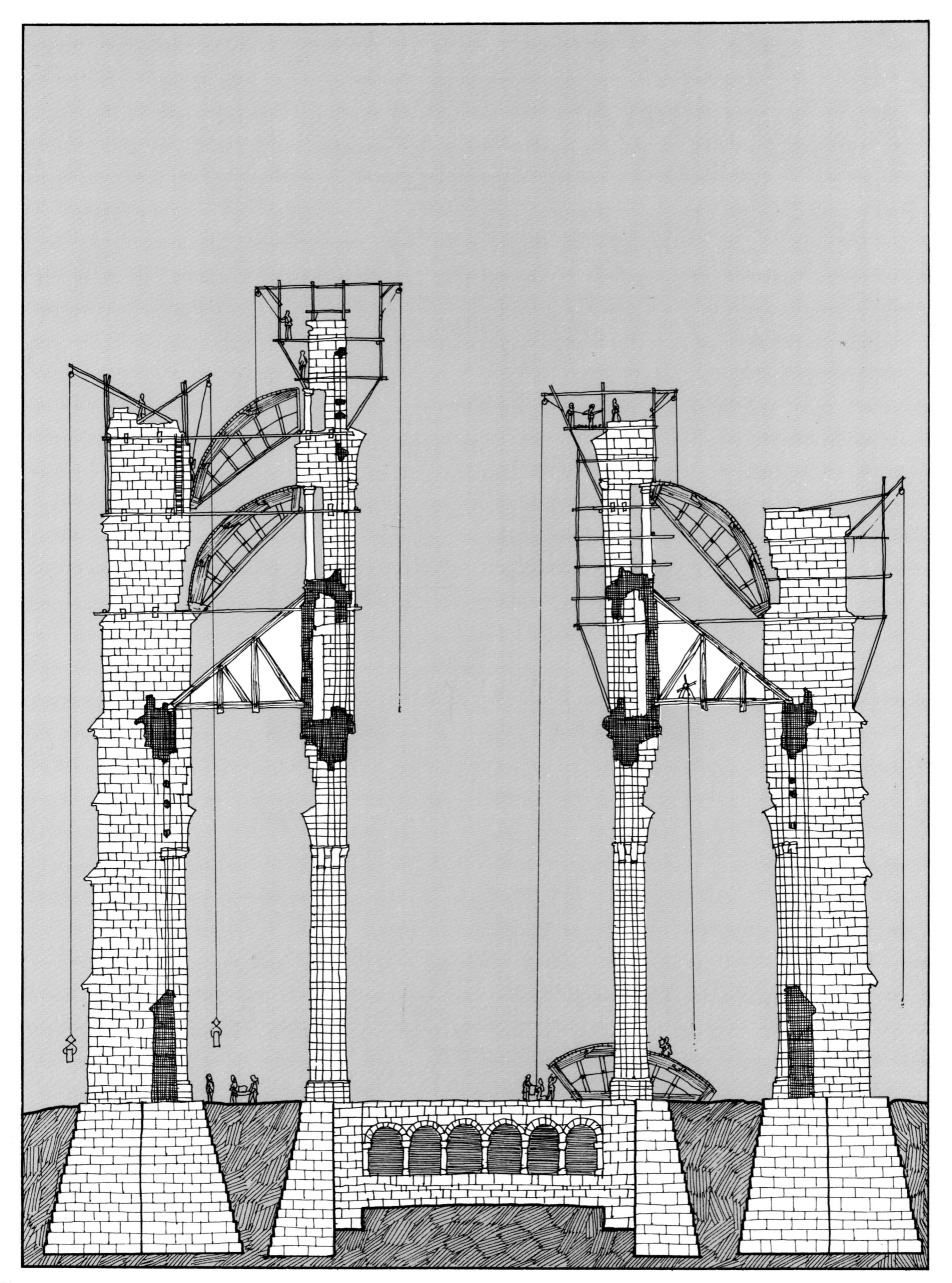

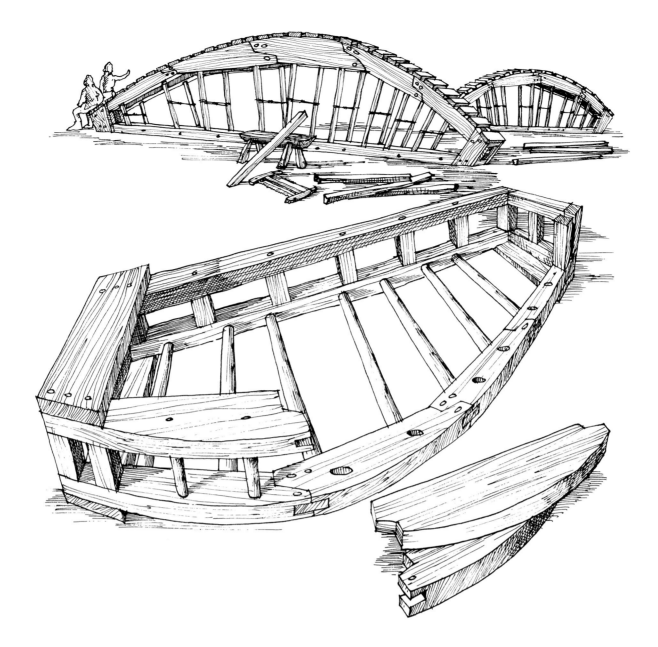

To build the flying buttresses it was first necessary to construct temporary wooden frames called centerings. These would support the weight of the stones and maintain the shape of the arch until the mortar was dry. These centerings were first built on the ground by the carpenters. Then they were hoisted into place and fastened to the pier at one end and to the buttress at the other. They acted as temporary flying buttresses until the stone arch was complete.

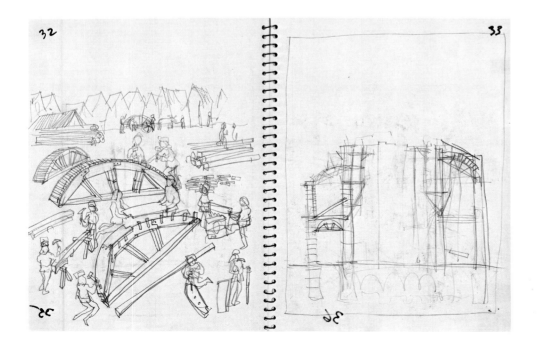

In the original sketch for the centering above, I showed lots of workers. But since I still had many drawings to make and time was running out, I gave them an early lunch break.

On the following double-page spread, I should have been more careful with the relationship between the gutter (the seam between the pages) and the drawing. In the original edition, the gutter sliced right through a buttress, which is both visually and structurally unsatisfactory. By simply enlarging the drawing slightly, I created a more natural break between the cathedral and the bishop's palace.

During the summer of 1270 the chapels in the apse and most of the piers and buttresses of the choir were finished. Much of the centering was also in place.

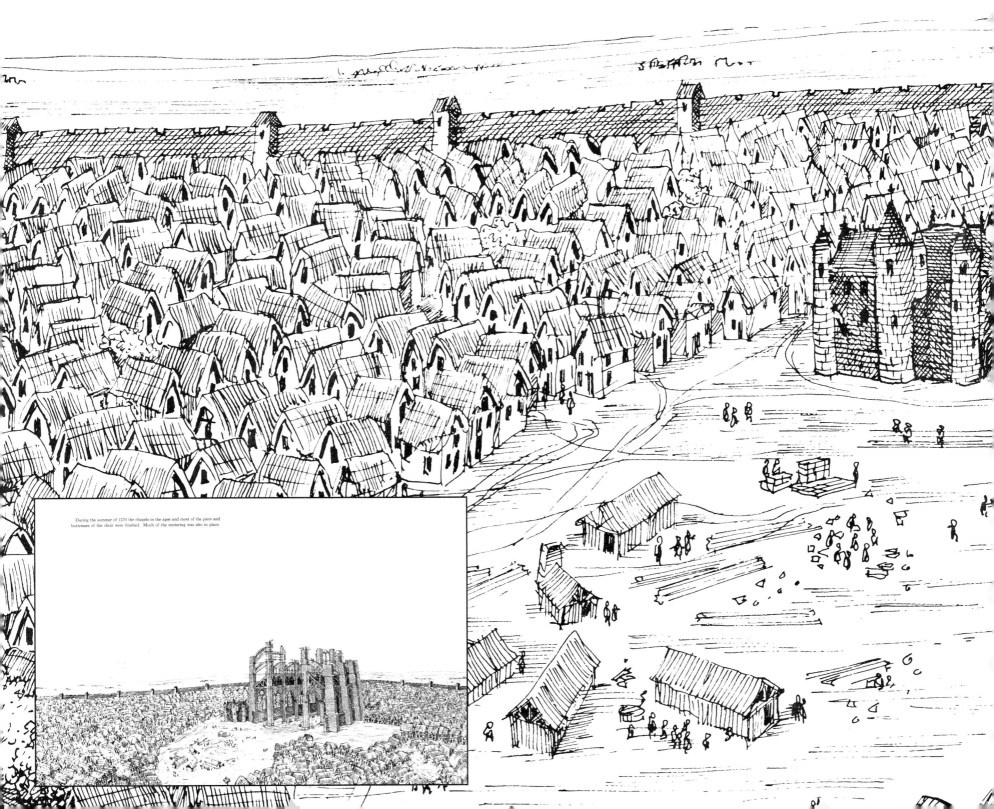

This drawing was originally intended to fill the page. But the more I worked on my people, the more difficult it became to distinguish them from the stone blocks they were carving. The finished drawing ended up being very small, though not small enough.

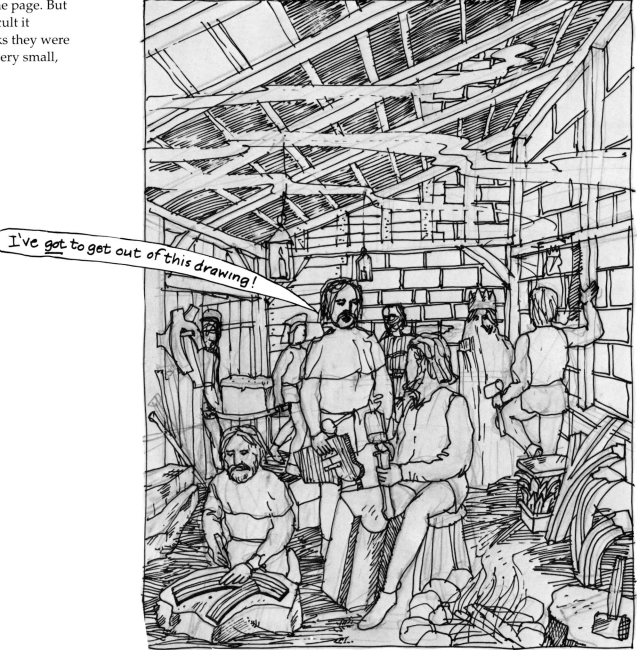

In November, as in every previous winter, the finished stonework was covered with straw and dung to prevent the frost from cracking the mortar before it had completely dried. Most of the masons went home for the winter because mortar work cannot be done in cold weather. Other work continued, however, for temporary workshops were built against the finished walls of the choir to house the stone cutters, who could no longer work outside. There they cut stones and tracery, carved capitals and sculptures in preparation for the return of the masons in the spring.

I've moved the winter scene to the right-hand page and lowered it slightly to strengthen its connection with the view on page 57. Now, when I turn from one page to the next, I get a stronger sense of the building growing. It's like a very short flip book. Very short.

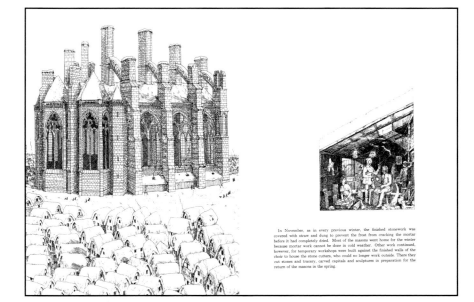

36

Sometimes it takes a while to get the right balance between drama and clarity. In these sketches I was trying to find the best point of view to ensure both. They all had the right feeling of vertigo, but none of them gave me enough information about the construction. In the end, I just pulled back a little.

The walls of the choir were constructed in three stages. First was the arcade of piers that rose eighty feet from the foundation. Above them was the triforium, a row of arches that went up another twenty feet in front of a narrow passageway. And the last stage was the clerestory, which consisted of sixty foot windows that reached right up to the roof.

Between 1270 and 1275 the walls of the choir and aisle were completed and work began on the roof.

If it isn't one thing, it's another. I was finally happy with the sense of height and with the details of construction. What bothers me twenty-five years later is the way the drawing sits on the page. Now I want the shapes of the empty spaces to contribute as much to the overall design as the drawn areas do. I've tried to improve the composition by enlarging and rotating the illustration and adjusting the text. What do you think? You'll have to cover the bottom part of this page to tell.

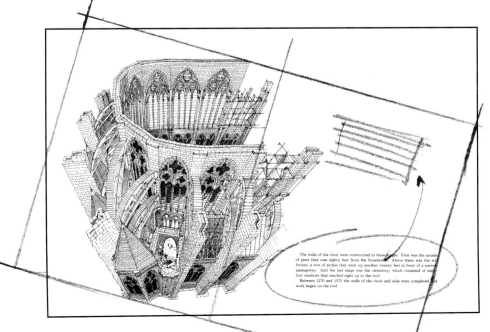

The roof was made up of a series of triangular frames or trusses. The carpenters first assembled each individual truss on the ground. The timbers were fastened together by the mortice-and-tenon method; holes called mortices were cut, into which the tongues or tenons of other pieces would then fit. After test assembling every part the truss was dismantled and hoisted piece by piece to the top of the walls. There it was reassembled and the entire frame was locked together with oak pegs. Nails were not used by the carpenters in the construction of the roof frame.

The first few beams were hoisted to the tops of the walls using pulleys hung from the scaffolding.

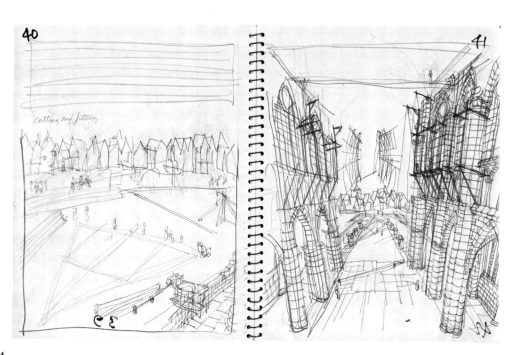

In this sketch the perspective is not only exaggerated but also wrong. The walls look like they're falling over. The little drawing in the middle is even more exaggerated, though in a way more accurate. In the finished illustration I still curved the walls slightly to emphasize their height.

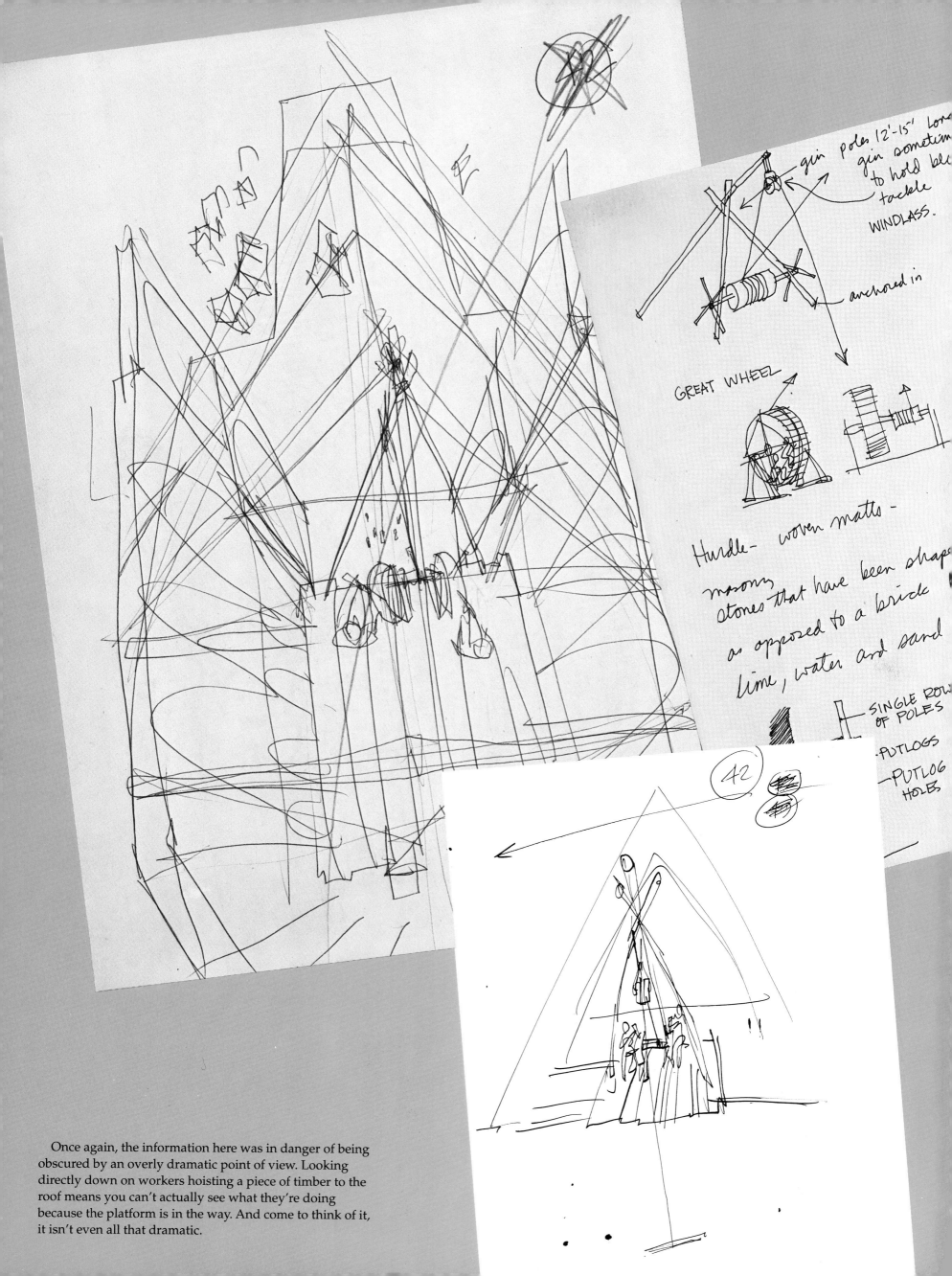

gin poles 12'-15' Lon[g]
gin sometim[es]
to hold ble[...]
tackle
WINDLASS.

anchored in

GREAT WHEEL

Hurdle - woven matts -

masonry
stones that have been shape[d]
as opposed to a brick

lime, water and sand

SINGLE ROW
OF POLES

PUTLOGS

PUTLOG
HOLES

42

Once again, the information here was in danger of being obscured by an overly dramatic point of view. Looking directly down on workers hoisting a piece of timber to the roof means you can't actually see what they're doing because the platform is in the way. And come to think of it, it isn't even all that dramatic.

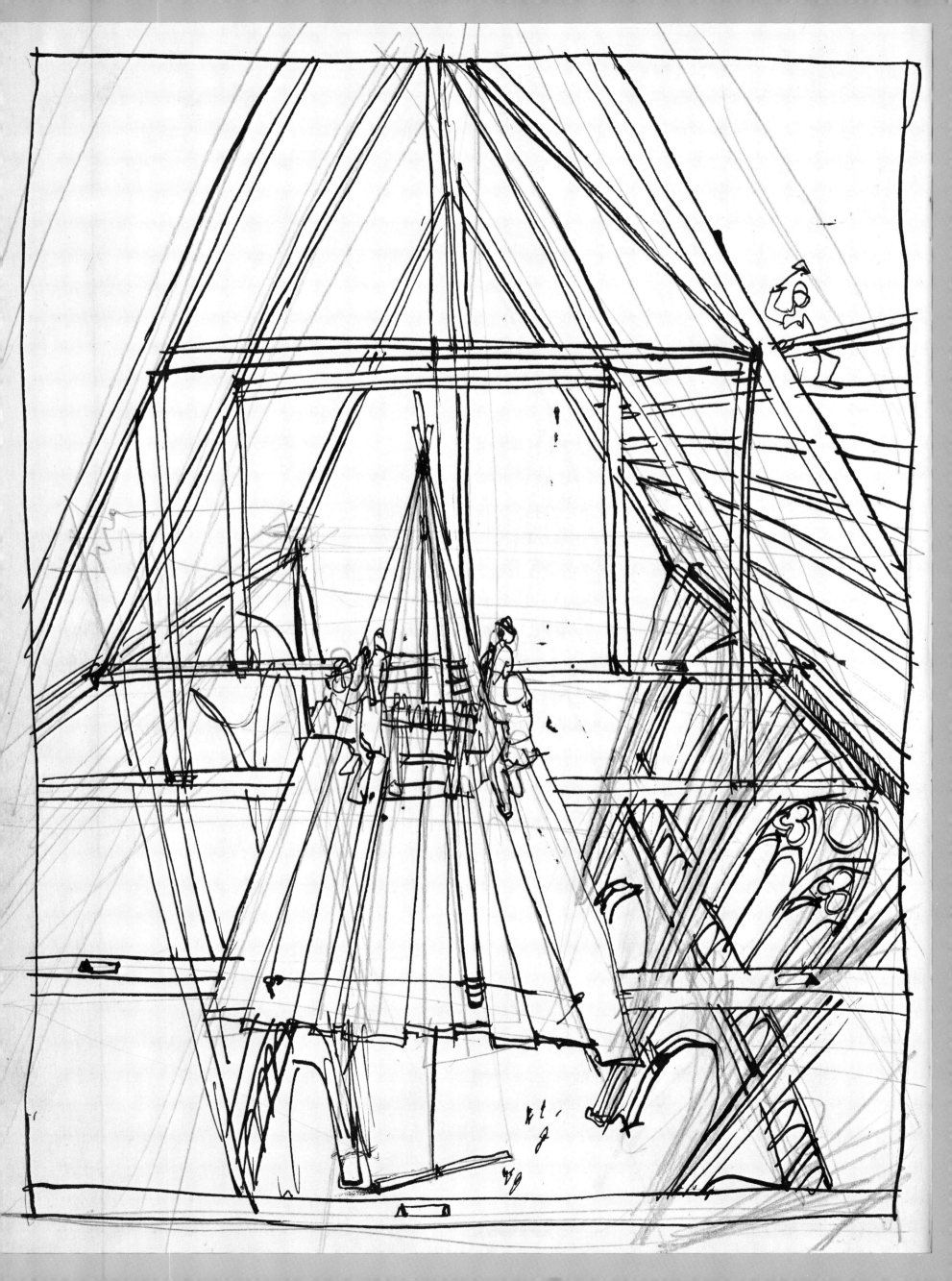

The face of the gargoyle is based on a photo of an old friend who will remain nameless. He was mimicking the opening in a cement trash container that had been sculpted to look like a tree trunk. I don't remember why, but he was pretty good at it. The other gargoyle is real and from Amiens.

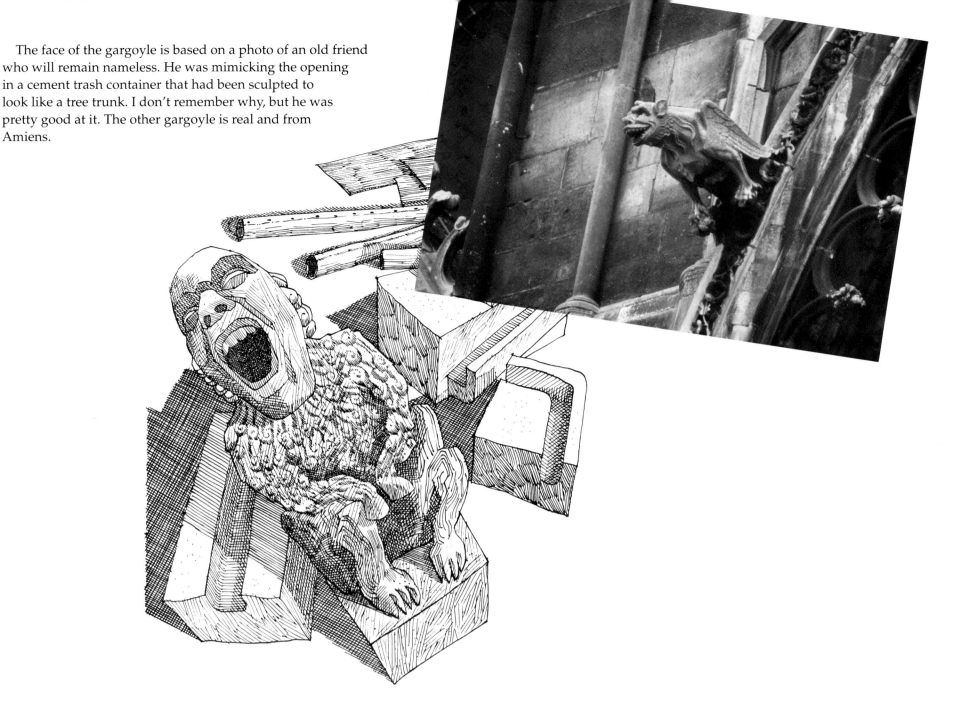

Once the beams were in place a windlass was set on top of them to hoist the rest of the timber and help in setting up the trusses.

Meanwhile, on the ground, the roofers were casting lead sheets that would cover the wooden frame, protecting it and the vaults from bad weather. They also cast the drain pipes and gutters. The stone cutters and sculptors carved the stone gutters and down spouts that were to be installed in the buttresses. These down spouts, through which the water from the roof fell to the ground, were carved to look like frightening creatures. They were called gargoyles and, when it rained, they would appear to be spitting water onto the ground below.

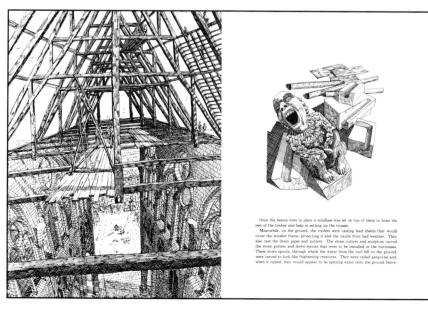

I've reversed the order of these two pages to make it easier to compare the final sketch on page 67 with the finished drawing on page 69. As you can see, the finished drawing has been printed backward. All the horizontal lines now drop precipitously, leading our eyes right off the edge of the page. Although this was the printer's mistake, I've kept it because it helps emphasize the uncertainty and danger of working at such great heights without a net. Thank you, printer.

The gargoyles were installed on the buttresses and connected to the gutters at the base of the roof by a channel along the top of the flying buttresses. Then large vats of pitch were hoisted up to the roof and the timber was coated to prevent it from rotting. Finally, as the sheets of lead were nailed to the framework, the edges were rolled to prevent any water from seeping in.

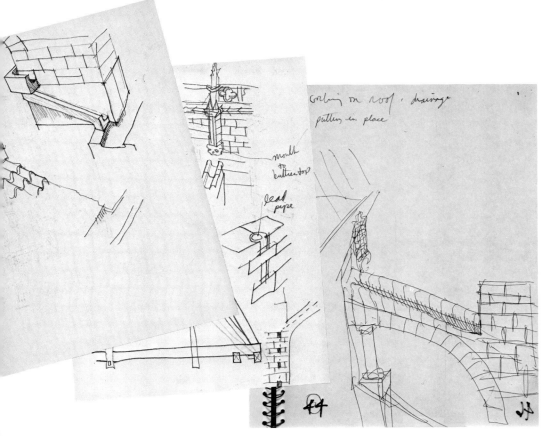

I had a number of sketches of gutters, downspouts, and roof details. In the end I settled for a simple cross section because it did the job and I was running out of time.

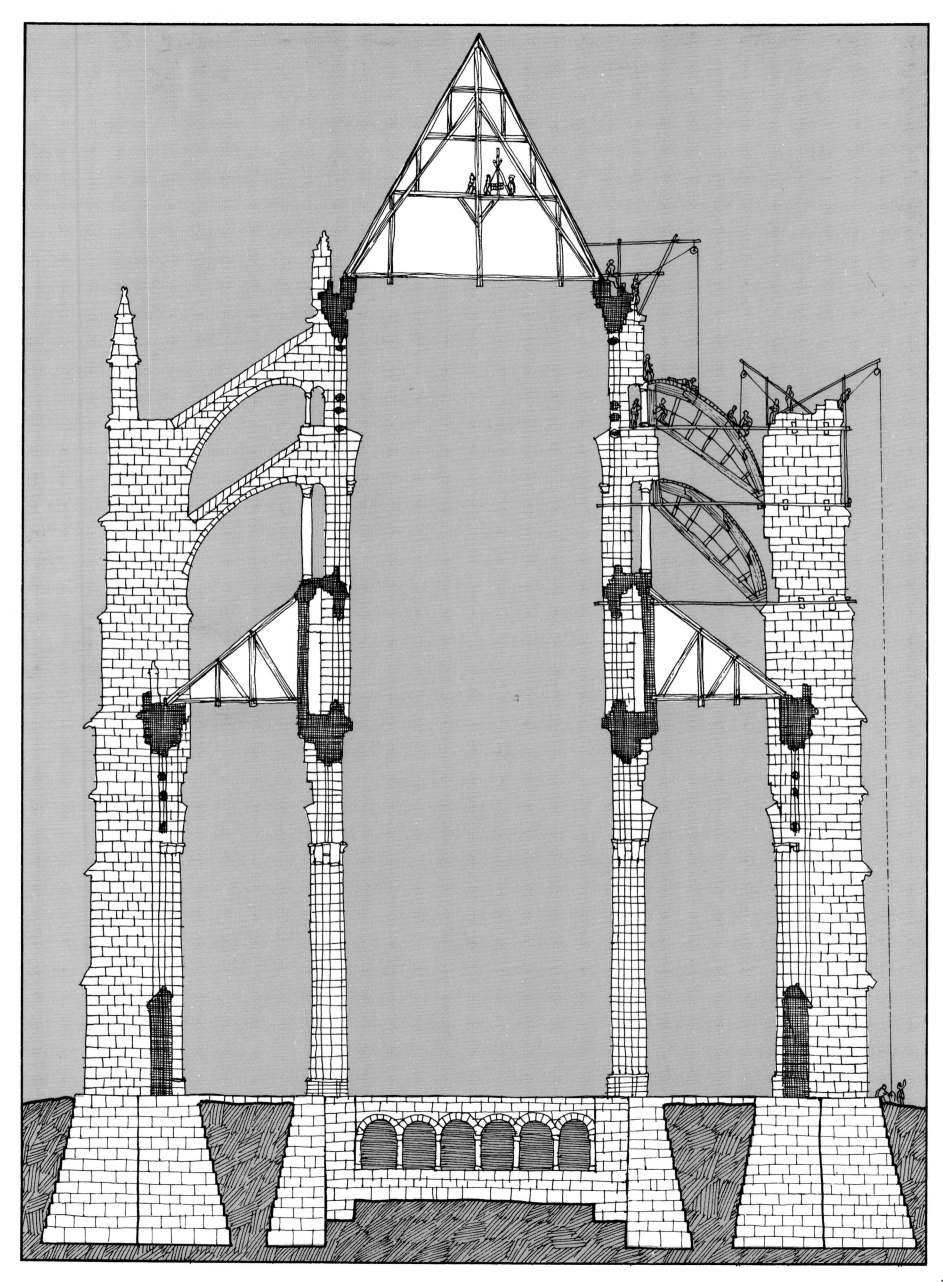

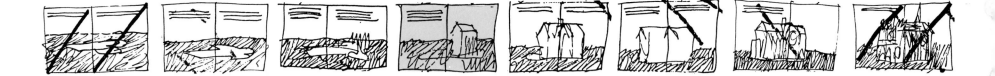

By 1280 the choir was ready for the construction of the vaulted ceiling and the foundation of the transept was begun. William, who was now too old to supervise the construction, was replaced by Robert of Cormont as master builder.

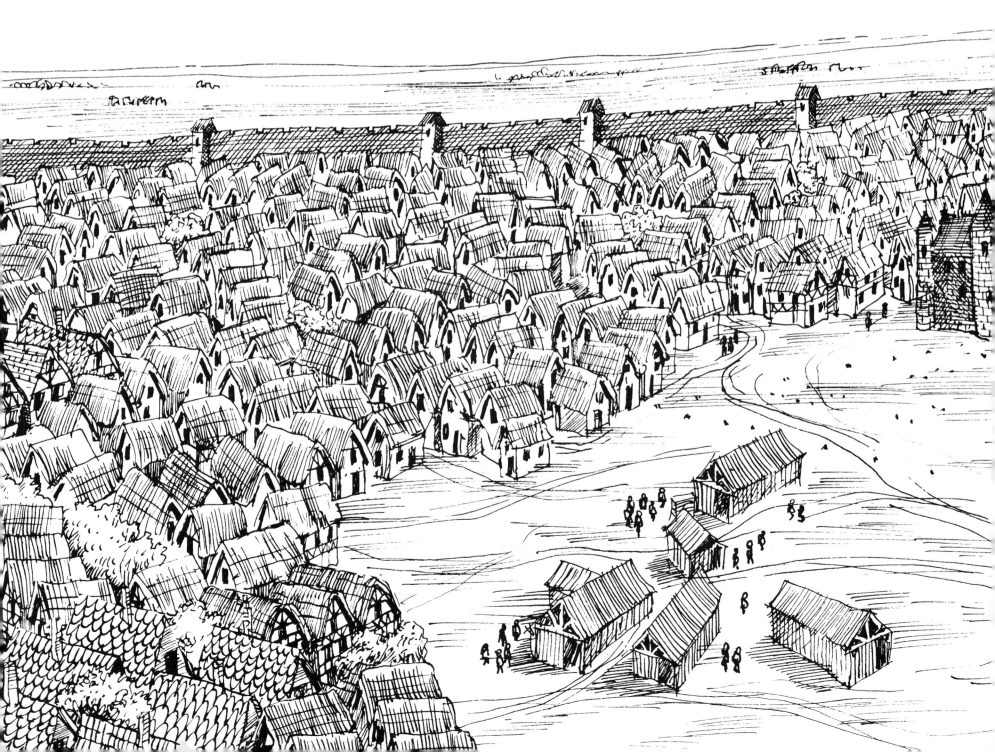

I was never very happy with this drawing. I wanted the building to be big, so I let it fill the page. But it always seemed squeezed in and cut off. Here, I've added a piece to the left-hand side. Even though the structure is now smaller, I think it feels larger because our eyes have a chance to climb more gradually toward the roof.

Here is a beautiful example of not reading my own text. This great wheel would never have been big enough for two men to stand inside it. Even leprechauns would have found it a tight fit. Scissors and glue to the rescue once again.

Two devices were used to lift the stones and concrete to the roof for the construction of the vaults. The first was the windlass and the second was the great wheel. The windlass, which had helped lift the timbers of the roof, was already in place and was used to raise the great wheel. The wheel was large enough so that one or two men could stand inside. Through its center ran a long axle to which the hoisting rope was fastened. As the men walked forward both the wheel and the axle turned, winding up the rope. This method enabled them to lift very heavy loads.

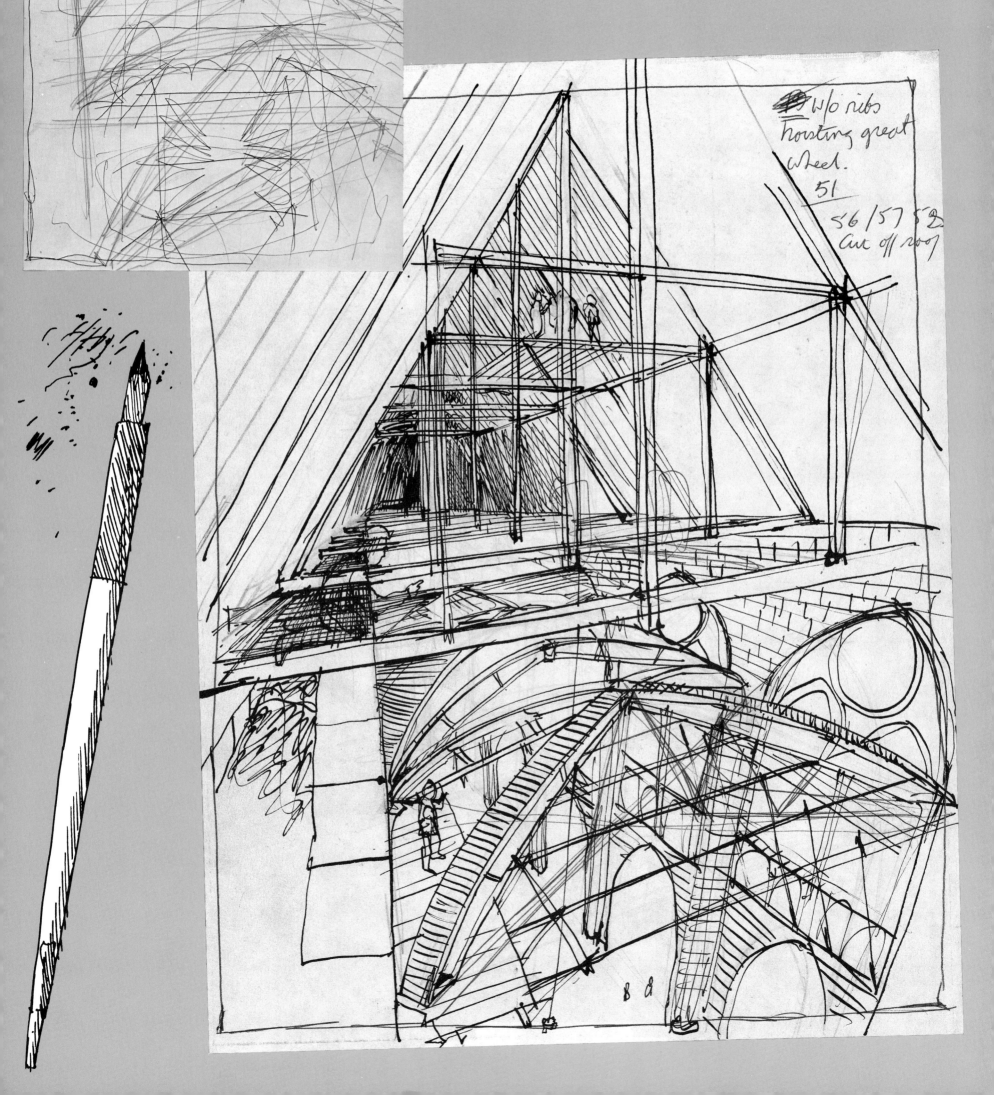

This little series gives a pretty good idea of the evolution of almost every drawing in the book, although a few of them did require three times as many sketches. Everything was going beautifully until I got to the great wheel (still shown here at its hamster-cage scale). But the size isn't the only problem. Using my own sloppy notes from page 66, I mistakenly wrapped the rope around the wheel instead of its axle.

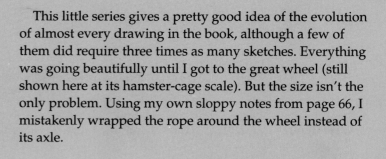

w/o ribs
hoisting great
wheel.
51
56 / 57 58
cut off roof

Although this arrangement might have been terrific for spinning salad, it offers no advantage whatsoever as a lifting device, and it would have been most uncomfortable for anyone standing inside the wheel should there have been a tug on the rope. The real problem, however, is that I didn't catch the mistake. At least not until after the first edition came out, by which time everyone else in the free world already had.

← NO

In order to construct the vaulted ceiling a wooden scaffold was erected connecting the two walls of the choir one hundred and thirty feet above ground. On the scaffolding wooden centerings like those used for the flying buttresses were installed. They would support the arched stone ribs until the mortar was dry, at which time the ribs could support themselves. The ribs carried the webbing, which was the ceiling itself. The vaults were constructed one bay at a time, a bay being the rectangular area between four piers.

It was during the construction of the scaffolding and centerings that the bishop of Chutreaux died. Work stopped for seven days. The bishop was buried on the fourteenth of September in 1281, twenty-eight years after construction had first begun. After a long service his body was placed in a new tomb in the old crypt. On the twenty-first of September Roland of Clermont was installed as the new bishop of Chutreaux.

With appropriate speed and humility, I glued a new wheel over the original drawing in such a way as to minimize any redrawing. What I should also have done was slide the wheel to the right to show the rope coiled around the axle. Oh, well. I'm sure that even in medieval France hindsight was *vingt-vingt*.

The following drawing was originally confined to the left-hand page facing another cross section. Looking at that spread now and rereading the text, I think I should have ditched the cross section and let the buttresses and town below fill the space. The variety would have been welcome and the view much more dramatic. Incidentally, in adding to the town to show you what I mean, I've changed the density a little. There should have been more open spaces within the walls.

When work resumed, the flying buttresses of the choir were completed and the centering was readied for the first stones of the vault.

When work resumed, the flying buttresses of the choir were completed, and the centering was readied for the first stones of the vault.

~~One by one~~ *Next* the cut stones of the ribs, called voussoirs, were hoisted *one by one* onto the centering and ^ mortared into place by the masons. Finally the keystone was lowered into place to lock the ribs together at the crown, the highest point of the arch.

In all my books, I've tried to make the words and the pictures work together as seamlessly as possible. This means the writing isn't truly finished until all the drawings are done and vice versa. Things often get shifted around — a word here, a sketch there — right up to the deadline and sometimes, to an editor's dismay, slightly beyond.

Incidentally, the bird's nest in this series of drawings appeared quite spontaneously. This kind of thing is not unusual when you've been drawing for eight weeks straight.

The carpenters then installed pieces of wood, called lagging, that spanned the space between two centerings. On top of the lagging the masons laid one course or layer of webbing stones. The lagging supported the course of webbing until the mortar was dry. The webbing was constructed of the lightest possible stone to lessen the weight on the ribs. Two teams, each with a mason and a carpenter, worked simultaneously from both sides of a vault — installing first the lagging and then the webbing. When they met in the center the vault was complete. The vaulting over the aisle was constructed in the same way and at the same time.

When the mortar in the webbing had set, a four-inch layer of concrete was poured over the entire vault to prevent any cracking between the stones. Once the concrete had set, the lagging was removed and the centering was lowered and moved onto the scaffolding of the next bay. The procedure was repeated until eventually the entire choir was vaulted.

Although I don't remember exactly why, each of the three preceding drawings was completely redone to correct the problem with the great wheel. And the scale of the bucket is *still* wrong. It looks like a medieval hot tub.

By the first of May, 1302, the transept and most of its vaulting was complete. Since this was an annual holiday, instead of working everyone attended the May Day celebration and fair at the cathedral.

This is the first of the overview drawings that uses the last one in the series as its base. On the original artwork, you could actually see where I had pasted a piece of paper over the photo print. When it was printed, though, the "ghost" disappeared. I've reintroduced it here just to remind you of the process.

By this time the glass makers had started working on the beautiful colored glass for the huge windows. They made the glass from a mixture of beechwood ash and washed sand that was melted at high temperatures. After different kinds of metals were added to the molten mixture for color, the glass makers scooped up a ball of molten glass on the end of a hollow pipe and blew it up like a balloon. By cutting the end off the balloon and spinning the pipe quickly the glass opened up into a flat circular shape. It was then removed from the pipe and allowed to cool.

The glass was cut into a square shape with a grozing iron, a steel rod with a sharp point at one end, to the right shape and size for the window. The pattern for the window had been drawn on a whitewashed bench so that the glass could be cut to the exact size and shape simply by laying it over the pattern.

After several pieces of glass had been cut, they were joined by strips of lead. Single pieces of glass were usually no larger than eight inches by eight inches, but sections as large as thirty inches square could be made when held together by the lead. These sections were inserted between stone mullions and the reinforcing bars to create windows as high as sixty feet.

The only information I had on glassmaking was a step-by-step list from a book on the history of technology. So I just converted it into a visual list. Here, to make the sequence a little clearer, I have rearranged the workers slightly and given them more space.

While the windows were being installed, plasterers covered the underside of the vault and painted red lines on it to give the impression that all the stones of the web were exactly the same size. They were eager for the web to appear perfect even if no one could see the lines from the ground.

Stone cutters and sculptors finished the moldings and capitals while masons laid the stone slabs that made up the floor. They created a maze pattern in the floor. Finding one's way to the center of the maze was considered as worthy of God's blessing as making the long pilgrimage through the countryside that so many had to make in order to worship in a cathedral such as Chutreaux's.

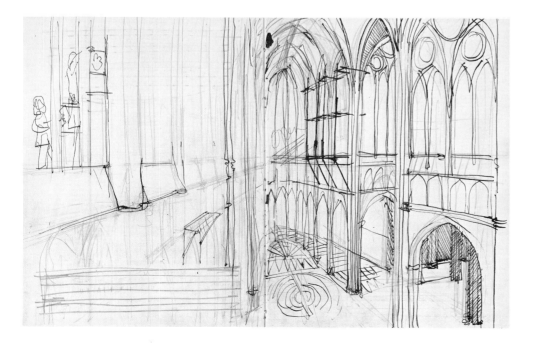

My original intent was to illustrate all the elements of the text in one dramatic double-page drawing. But I gave up when I couldn't find a place to put the text that wouldn't have obliterated at least one of those elements.

In 1306 work stopped again, this time because the chapter had run out of money. It was decided that the best way to raise the necessary funds was to exhibit the remains of Saint Germain. The people of northern France and southern England would gladly pay to see such relics, and so they were displayed for five years until enough money had been collected. It wasn't until 1330 that the nave was finally completed.

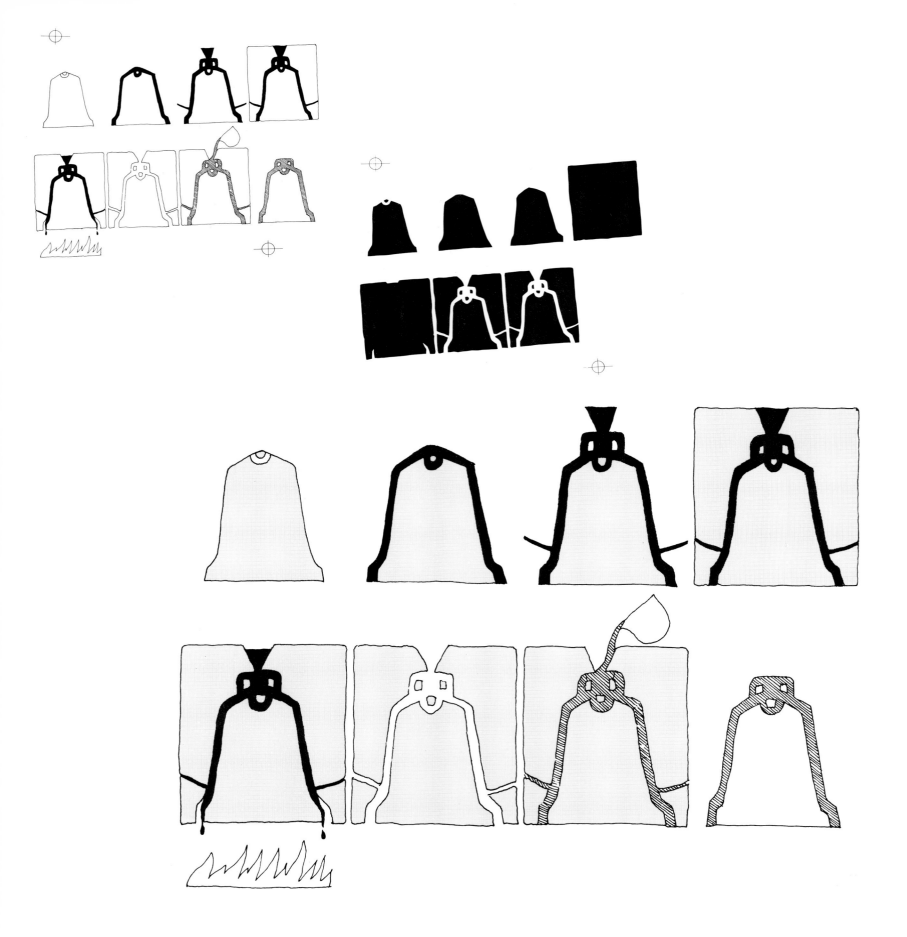

At the foundry in Chutreaux four large bells were cast in bronze. A model of the bell, as if it were solid, was first made of clay and plaster of Paris. It was covered then with a coat of wax of the same thickness that the finished bell was to be, and the required decoration on the outside of the bell was carved on the wax. This was then covered by a layer of clay and plaster compound.

When the whole construction was heated the wax melted and ran out, leaving a cavity between the outer shell and the core. This was the mold into which molten bronze was poured. When the metal cooled the mold was destroyed and the bell was prepared for shipment to the building.

The tracery of the rose window for the front of the cathedral was carefully cut according to the plans. Voussoirs were carved to form the arched gables over each of the three front doors and a tympanum — a semicircular sculptured panel — was carved to go above each of the doors.

459
vol 5

wood frame
cover w/ lead sheets.

TILE

The spire was a difficult shape to play with, which is
hardly surprising when you consider that its main function
is to point upward. Armed with notes and photographs and
undeterred by the geometrically obvious, I tried sneaking up
on the spire from various points of view in my quest for
drama.

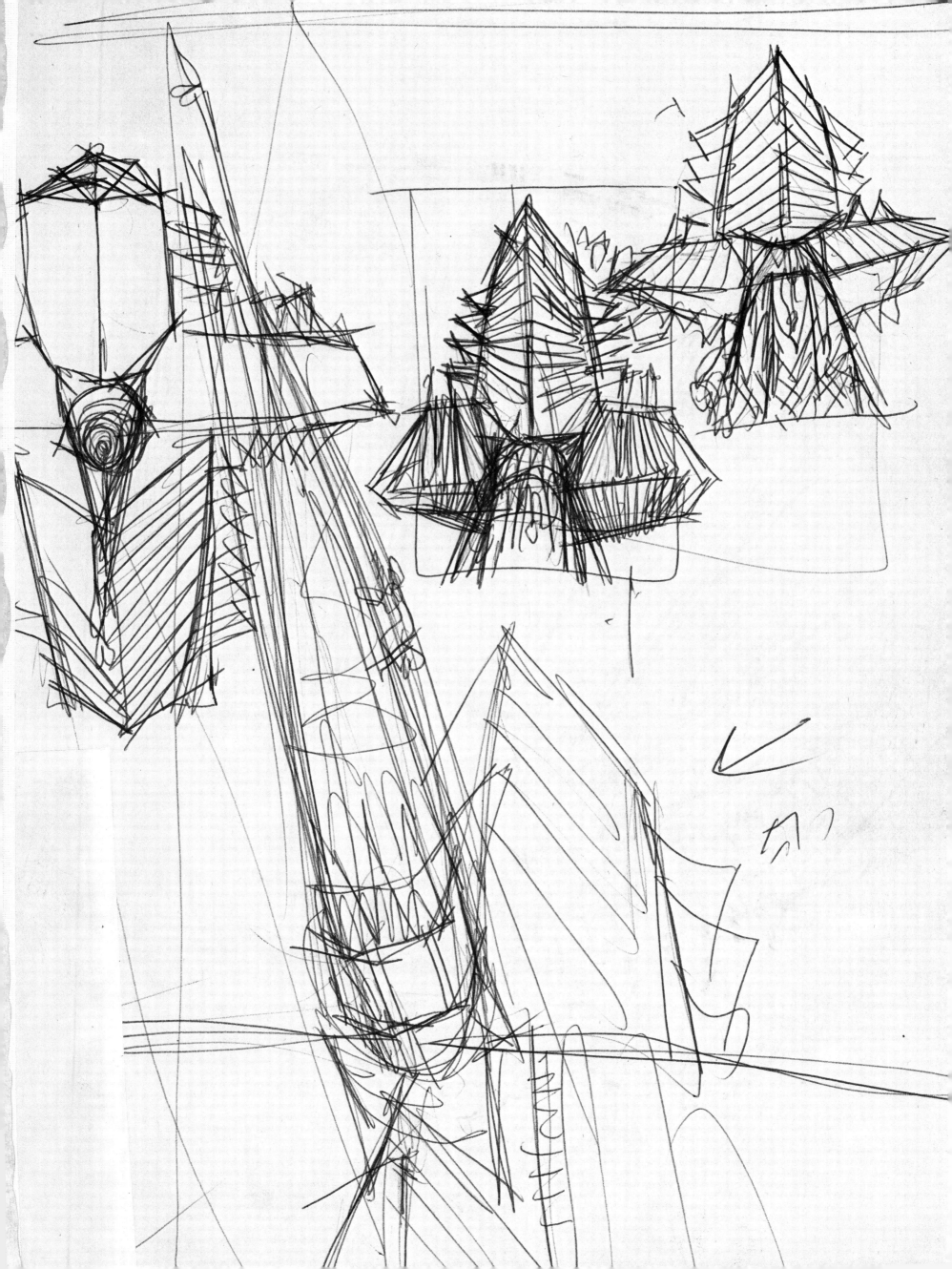

By 1331 the carpenters and roofers had completed work on the spire, which rose above the crossing of the nave and the transept. The spire was a wood frame structure covered with sheets of lead and highly decorated with sculptures and ornaments.

Meanwhile, in the carpenters' workshop the doors were being built. The center door alone was almost twenty-five feet high, made of heavy planks of wood and joined with cross-ribs. A blacksmith made all the nails for the door and a master metal worker made the bolts and locks and hinges.

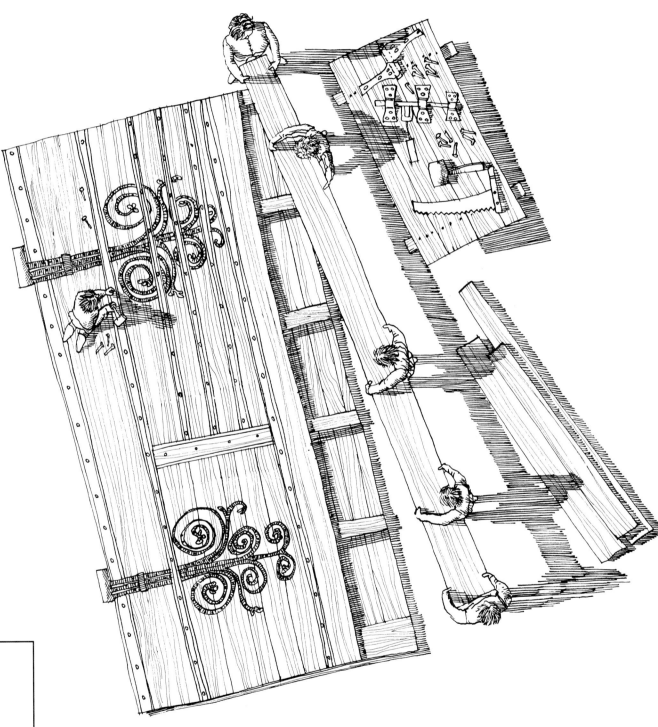

In the end, I admitted defeat and kept it simple. But I'm back and I've made a few changes. By not letting the complete spire fit on the page, I can emphasize its enormous scale. By disconnecting it from a secure base, I can make it seem a little less structurally reliable. Finally, if I eliminate the original symmetry with a shift to the left and a slight tilt, this becomes as much a drawing about height and danger as it is about a spire. And if you feel bad about not seeing the whole thing, just turn the page.

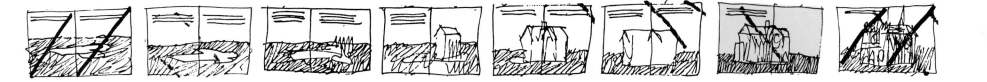

In 1332 work was in progress on the west end or front of the cathedral. The construction of the towers was supervised by the master craftsman Etienne of Gaston. He had replaced Robert of Cormont, who died in 1329 after falling from the scaffolding of the vaults.

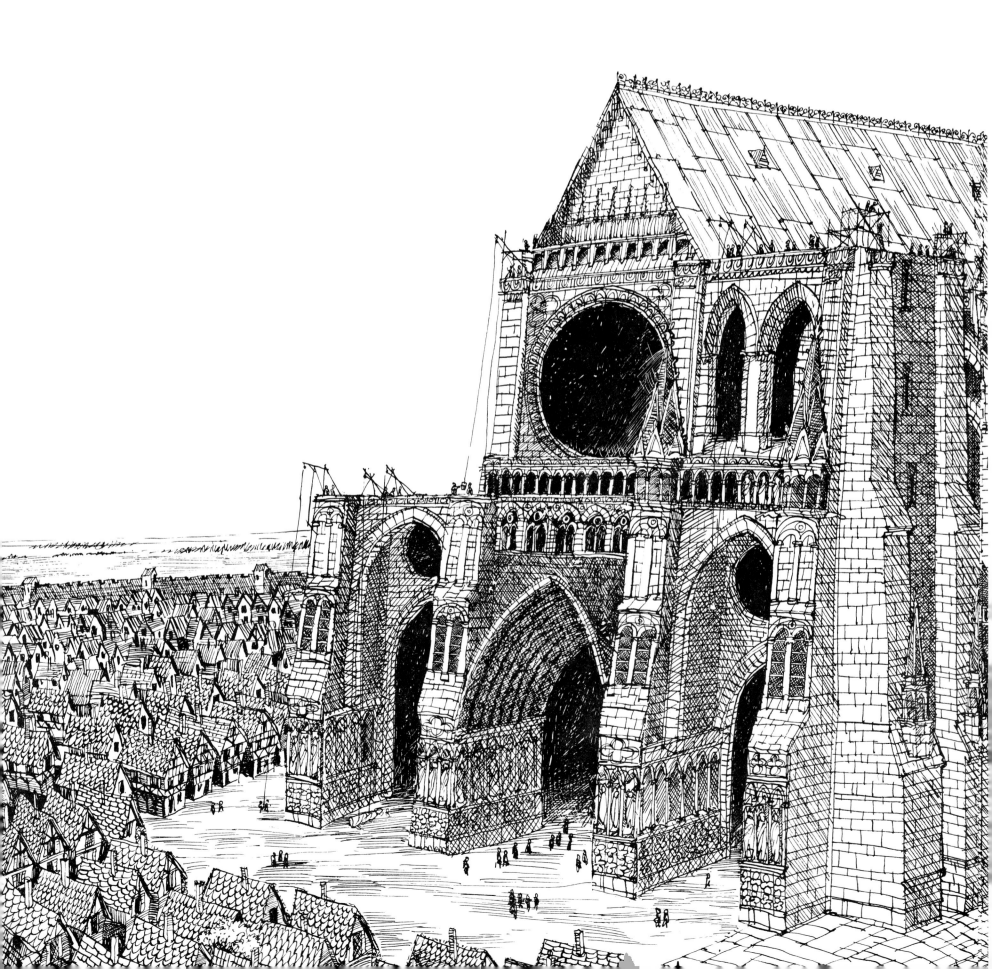

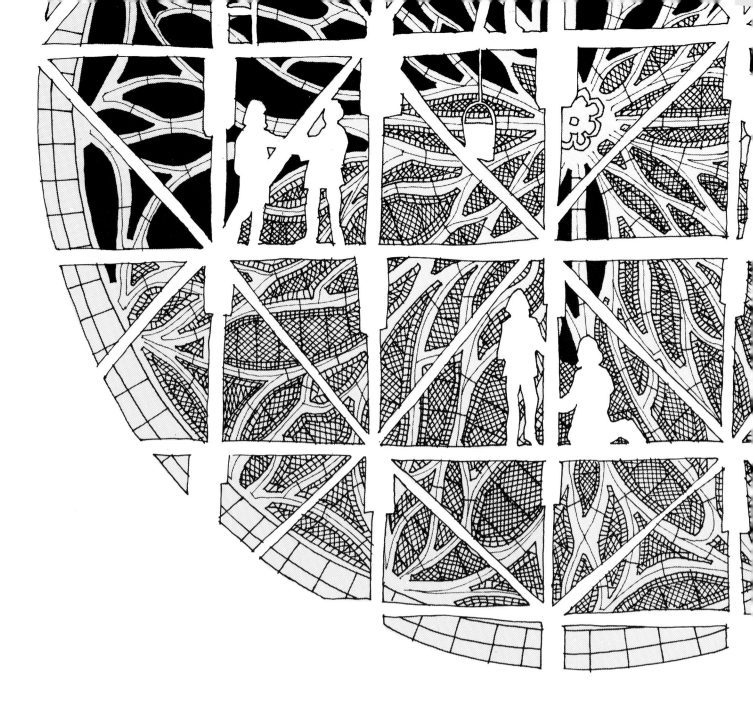

A heavy timber framework was constructed in the north tower. From it the bells were carefully hoisted and fastened into place. Four ropes hung down from the bells. When they were pulled the bells would rock back and forth, causing the hammers inside to hit the sides of the bells. The ringing could be heard for miles.

The masons put together the pieces of the rose window and installed the tympanums and voussoirs over the doors. Then the window makers came and filled the rose window's thirty-two-foot diameter with hundreds of pieces of colored glass.

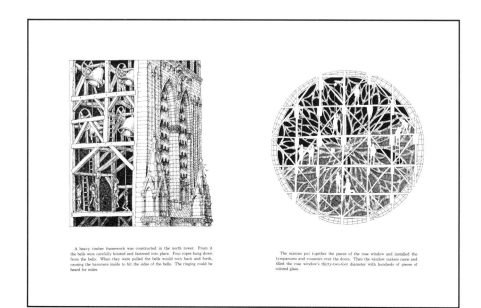

A heavy timber framework was constructed in the north tower. From it the bells were carefully hoisted and fastened into place. Four ropes hung down from the bells. When they were pulled the bells would rock back and forth, causing the hammers inside to hit the sides of the bells. The ringing could be heard for miles.

The masons put together the pieces of the rose window and installed the tympanums and voussoirs over the doors. Then the window makers came and filled the rose window's thirty-two-foot diameter with hundreds of pieces of colored glass.

This spread was adequate but dull. Since we are about to see a complete view of both towers and the rose window in the next spread, I've decided to move in a little closer.
Without losing any important information, I now have shapes that create a much more dramatic composition.

By midsummer of 1338, the last pieces of sculpture had been hoisted into their niches. The cathedral was finished. On August 19 the bishop and the chapter led a great procession through the narrow streets of Chutreaux, returning to the grand, new cathedral with the entire population of the city for a service of thanksgiving.

Above is the first sketch of the townspeople packed into the cathedral for the celebration of its completion. To the right is a photograph of the nave of Amiens, which helped me get the proportions of the various levels right before moving on to the final sketch. As with all the drawings, once the final sketch had been prepared and double-checked, it was placed on a light table. I then traced it on a sheet of drawing paper in pencil. Finally, using a dip pen and a bottle of ink, I added all the cross-hatching, erasing the pencil lines as I went. If this sounds like an incredibly tedious process, let me assure you — it is.

The drawings for *Cathedral* were among my first serious attempts at working with pen and ink. They are understandably timid, especially when it comes to shadows and shading. In the case of the drawing to the right, that reticence is a good thing. Notice the shafts of light pouring through the windows along the left-hand side of the nave. If you flip back to page 32, the plan of the cathedral, you'll see that this wall actually faces north — a direction not generally known for its strong direct sunlight. Whoops.

Huge colored banners had been hung from the triforium and all the candles on the piers were lit. As the choir began to sing, the building filled with beautiful sounds and the people, most of them grandchildren of the men who had laid the foundation, were filled with tremendous awe and a great joy.

For eighty-six years the townspeople had shared one goal and it had at last been reached.

The people of Chutreaux had constructed the longest, widest, highest, and most beautiful cathedral in all of France.

In the original edition, the cathedral on the last page, the one I drew in France, was jammed against the right-hand edge. When we decided to use this drawing for the dust jacket, I had to add about half an inch of town so that it would wrap around the front cover. It seems obvious to me now that I should have used the revised art inside the book as well. Oh, well. *C'est la vie,* I guess.

The people of Chutreaux had constructed the longest, widest, highest, and most beautiful cathedral in all of France.

Shoot same reduction
as before but note new art
for jacket in this area

BLEED SIDES & BOTTOM

18"

78/9

75%

Sometime in June 1973 a proof of *Cathedral* arrived in a large envelope. There was no hard cover yet, just eighty pages stitched together and wrapped in a dust jacket. This almost complete version of the book, produced primarily for the sales staff, gave me one final opportunity to make adjustments before the presses rolled. And I would have, if only I had known what to adjust. Technical mistakes, like that pesky "great wheel," I learned about and corrected within months. However, the more subtle aspects of telling a story through pictures I'm still working on. Who would have thought that twenty-five years later I'd get another chance to make changes? I can't wait for the fiftieth anniversary.

AISLE
The part of a church that runs parallel to the main areas — nave, choir, and transept — and is separated from them by an arcade.

APSE
The circular or angular end of a church, usually the east end.

BUTTRESS
Sometimes called a buttress pier, this is the large stone pier that rises across the aisle from the pier and is connected to the pier by a flying buttress.

CAPITAL
The form, usually of stone, that supplies the visual transition between the top of a column and whatever the column supports.

CATHEDRAL
A church of any size that contains the Cathedra or bishop's chair.

CENTERING
The timber framework that supports the stones of an arch until the mortar between them is dry.

CHOIR
The section of the church east of the transept that is sometimes raised above the level of the nave. It is called the choir because traditionally this is where the choir stands to sing during the service.

CLERESTORY
The topmost part of the church building whose windows illuminate the central portion of the interior space.

CROWN
The highest part of the arch, where the keystone is located.

CRYPT
A lower level, usually below ground, that is used for burial or as a chapel.

FLYING BUTTRESS
A stone arch that carries the thrust of the vault to the buttress.

GOTHIC ARCHITECTURE
The architectural style that developed in northern France and spread throughout Europe between 1150 and 1400. Large areas were covered by stone vaults supported on slender stone piers. By reducing the structure to piers the area between them could be and usually was filled with glass. The weight and pressure of the pointed vault is concentrated at the points where the vault touches the piers. This load is then split up. Some is carried down the pier to its foundation; the rest is carried across the flying buttress to the buttress and then down to its foundation. The most common features of Gothic architecture are the pointed arches and vaults, the large amounts of glass in the walls, and an overall feeling of great height.

HURDLES
A movable work platform made of woven twigs.

KEYSTONE
The central locking stone at the top of an arch.

LAGGING
Temporary wooden planks or frames used to support the courses or layers of webbing stone until the mortar is dry.

MORTICE AND TENON
A method of fastening one piece of wood to another. A mortice or square hole is cut into one piece of wood while a tenon or projection the same size as the hole is cut on the end of the other piece. The tenon is then tapped into the mortice, locking the two together without nails.

MULLION
The narrow upright stone pier used to divide the panels of glass in a window.

NAVE
The central area of a church where the congregation usually stands.

PIER
The pillar or column that supports an arch.

RIB
The stone arch that supports and strengthens the vault.

ROMANESQUE ARCHITECTURE
The architectural style that developed between the end of the Roman Empire and around 1000 A.D. In church architecture the nave became higher and narrower and the many columns that supported the triforium, clerestory, and roof were replaced by a few large piers. The flat wooden ceilings of the earlier churches, which kept burning down, were gradually replaced by round stone vaults. The round arch and the vault are the most common features of Romanesque buildings.

TEMPLATE
The full-size wooden pattern used by the stone cutter when he has to cut many pieces of stone the same size and shape.

TRACERY
The decorative carved stonework of a medieval church window.

TRANSEPT
In a Latin cross plan as at Chutreaux, the section that crosses the nave, usually separating the nave and the choir.

TRIFORIUM
The arcaded story between the nave arcade and the clerestory.

TRUSS
A triangular wooden frame. The roof frame is constructed of a series of trusses fastened together.

TYMPANUM
The sculptural area enclosed by the arch above the doors of a cathedral.

VAULT
The form of construction, usually of brick or stone, that is based on the shape of the arch. Used for the most part as a ceiling or roof.

VOUSSOIRS
Blocks of stone cut in wedge shapes to form an arch.

WINDLASS
A machine for hoisting or hauling. In the Middle Ages this consisted of a horizontal wooden barrel with a long rope fastened to it. The barrel was supported at both ends. When it was turned the rope would gradually be wound up around it.

Walter Lorraine (wr) Books

Printed in the United States of America
NBB 10 9 8 7 6 5 4 3 2 1

Library of Congress Cataloging-in-Publication Data

Macaulay, David.
  Building the book Cathedral / by David Macaulay.
    p.   cm.
  ISBN 0-395-92147-3
  1. Macaulay, David.   Cathedral.   2. Cathedrals.
3. Architecture, Gothic.   I. Title.
    NA4830.M317   1999
    726.6—dc21   99-17975
                                                 CIP